# The Children's Media Yearbook 2025

The Children's Media
FOUNDATION

The Children's Media Yearbook is a publication of The Children's Media Foundation

Director, Greg Childs

Administrator, Jacqui Wells

The Children's Media Foundation
15 Briarbank Rd
London
W13 0HH

info@thechildrensmediafoundation.org

First published 2025

© Hannie Kirkham, Laura Sinclair and Dr Ashley Woodfall for editorial material and selection

© Individual authors and contributors for their contributions

All rights reserved. No part of this publication may be reproduced, stored in a retrieval system, or transmitted, in any form or by any means, without the prior permission in writing of The Children's Media Foundation, or as expressly permitted by law, or under terms agreed with the appropriate reprographics rights organisation. You must not circulate this book in any other binding or cover.

Cover and book design by Rebekkah Silver

ISBN 978-1-9161353-7-6

# Contents

| | |
|---|---|
| Foreword<br>*Baroness Anne Longfield* | 5 |
| Editors' Welcome<br>*Hannie Kirkham, Laura Sinclair & Dr Ashley Woodfall* | 7 |
| The Children's Media Foundation: Chair's Report<br>*Anna Home OBE* | 9 |
| Be Positive: This Is An Opportunity For Change<br>*Colin Ward* | 11 |
| Jackanory At 60!<br>*Dr Diane Charlesworth* | 15 |
| I'll Tell You A Story, About Jackanory…<br>*Jeremy Swan* | 19 |
| A Box Of Delights<br>*Richard Marson* | 22 |
| Silly Matters: 50 Years Of Aardman<br>*Sarah Cox* | 25 |
| Milkshake! – A Preschool Institution<br>*Nick Wilson* | 27 |
| 30 Years Of Sony PlayStation: A Revolution In Play And Youth Culture<br>*Dr Carla Sousa & Ivan Barroso* | 30 |
| The Legacy Of Mary Field<br>*Anna Home OBE* | 34 |
| Tom Rides On: A Review<br>*Mary Field CBE* | 36 |
| 'Linear TV Is Dead?' Or: How I Learned To Stop Worrying And Love YouTube<br>*Colin Ward* | 40 |
| TVs With Wings And Other Creatures: Imagining The Future Of TV<br>*Dr Cassie Brummitt & Professor Elizabeth Evans* | 43 |
| International Understanding<br>*Greg Childs OBE* | 47 |
| Reading The Runes<br>*Jackie Edwards* | 50 |
| Children's Documentary: A Call To Preserve Real Stories<br>*Dr Tatyana Terzopoulos* | 53 |
| Play To Platform: Roblox Is Shaping The Future Of Kids' Digital Experience<br>*David Kleeman* | 57 |
| Trends In Kids' Content<br>*Karolina Kaminska* | 61 |
| Animating Minds Project: Age-Appropriate Impact Of Children's Media<br>*Professor Tim Smith, Alisa Musatova, Dr Claire Essex & Dr Rachael Bedford* | 66 |

| | |
|---|---|
| Pablo: Next Level. What We Do Matters<br>*Gráinne McGuinness* | 69 |
| Maddie + Triggs: It's Amazing What You Hear When You Take The Time To Listen<br>*Colm Tobin* | 72 |
| Ultra Access: Unlocking The Magic Of TV<br>*Rebecca Atkinson* | 75 |
| More Than Metrics: Youth Marketing For Passions And Fandoms<br>*Maxine Fox & Sam Clough* | 79 |
| Battle For The Boys: Evolving Masculinity On-Screen<br>*Dr Yalda T Uhlis* | 83 |
| From Surface To Substance: Personality Is The Future Of Engagement<br>*Lea Magnano* | 86 |
| Real-Time Magic: How AniMotion Live Is Redefining Character Engagement<br>*Richard Chaney* | 89 |
| Time For BeddyByes<br>*John Rice* | 92 |
| Reaching Young Audiences: Best Practice From Denmark<br>*Dr Eva Novrup Redvall* | 94 |
| Inclusive Storytelling: Writing For Maddie + Triggs<br>*Jayne Kirkham* | 97 |
| Are Tech Platforms Taking Over Family Life?<br>*Professor Sonia Livingstone & Alexandra Evans* | 100 |
| Preschoolers And YouTube/Kids<br>*Dr Jane O'Connor* | 103 |
| AI In Childhood: Striking The Balance Between Innovation And Safeguarding<br>*Dr Amanda Gummer* | 105 |
| Rethinking Digital Safety: Inclusion, Rights And A Child's Best Interests<br>*Professor Helen Sandberg & Professor Olu Jenzen* | 108 |
| Remembering Julie Stevens<br>*Paul R. Jackson* | 112 |
| Remembering Peter Murphy<br>*Sue Nott* | 114 |
| Contributors | 115 |

# Foreword

**Baroness Anne Longfield**, former Children's Commissioner for England

Television has been a feature of childhood for over 60 years and video games for well over 40 years. Yet the amount of screentime consumed by children has only recently become a national debate and cause for concern. Smartphones or tablets have become ubiquitous in most children's lives, and how children consume media has inevitably changed.

We are all searching for the right balance between the time children spend online and the creative and fun benefits of the digital world. At a time when there are more children with unhealthy weight and mental health problems, that should include encouraging children to switch off and spend more time enjoying the benefits of play in the outside world. But it also means making sure children can have the freedom, and are safe, to access the huge opportunities for learning and play provided through high-quality and diverse media.

If we want to see thriving childhoods, we should always make sure children have both the freedom and support that they need to play, alongside the freedom to learn and be entertained in ways that encourage their creativity, which challenge them, and which are fun.

# THE CHILDREN'S MEDIA CONFERENCE
## 8-9-10 JULY 2025

The Children's Media Conference is the UK's premier meeting place for the children's content industries.

CMC returns to Sheffield in July for three days of industry content – with access to all of CMC's keynotes, sessions and networking.

### Opening Keynote
CMC's Opening Keynote speaker is screenwriter, award-winning novelist and Waterstones Children's Laureate **Frank Cottrell-Boyce**. We have invited Frank in recognition of his unique contribution to the lives of children and young people, his passionate support of the people who make content for them and his razor-sharp observations on creativity, culture, content and the young. Don't miss Frank and don't miss the CMC.

### International Exchange
The CMC International Exchange is back LIVE in Sheffield on 8 July for a day of one-to-one meetings. It plays host to a wide range of broadcasters, co-producers, funders and investors from across the world keen to meet sellers of content and services.

Sign up to our email bulletin at
**www.thechildrensmediaconference.com**

- @childmediaconf
- the children's media conference
- the children's media conference
- childmediaconf
- contact@thechildrensmediaconference.com
- thechildrensmediaconference.com

# Editors' Welcome

**Hannie Kirkham**, Research and Strategy Manager, Oriel Square, **Laura Sinclair**, Doctoral Researcher, School of Journalism, Media and Culture, Cardiff University and **Dr Ashley Woodfall**, Associate Professor in Children's Media, Bournemouth University

*Warning. The following dialogue uses text and images from OpenAI's ChatGPT 2025, with surprisingly little poetic licence used by the editors. We believe that AI can be beneficial to the industry and our audiences when used 'wisely'.*

EDS: Ok ChatGPT, can you create a pitch for a children's TV show please?

CHATGPT: Sure! Here's a pitch for a children's TV show that balances entertainment with learning and emotional development.

Logline: When six-year-old Milo finds a magical backpack full of living emotions called the Moodies, every day becomes an adventure in understanding feelings, solving kid-sized problems, and learning how to be a great friend.

Premise: Milo is a kind and curious kid who one day discovers a mysterious backpack in his treehouse. Inside are the Moodies – tiny, colorful creatures, each representing a different emotion like Joy, Sadness, Anger, Worry and Confidence. Whenever Milo encounters a tough moment at school, at home, or on the playground, one (or more!) Moodies pop out to help him figure out what he's feeling and how to handle it.

EDS: Hmm that's too generic, and I think we might have some plagiarism at play. Can you try again?

CHATGPT: Got it – thanks for the honest feedback. Let's take a more original and distinctive angle. Here's a new, more unique pitch that avoids familiar tropes and delivers a fresh concept while still being age-appropriate and meaningful.

Logline: In the bizarre town of Oddfellow – where umbrellas grow on trees and time occasionally runs backward – 11-year-old Kip and his snail sidekick, Shelley, investigate the town's weekly "glitches" to keep everything weird... but not too weird.

Premise: Every Thursday in Oddfellow, something strange happens: the moon turns plaid, doors start singing opera, or everyone's thoughts appear as floating comic bubbles. Each week, Kip and Shelley investigate the latest mystery, meeting strange residents (like Ms. Nozzle, who communicates via smoke signals, or the Pancake Mayor) and slowly uncovering a layered, long-running mystery about Oddfellow's true origin.

EDS: Um, thanks for trying, ChatGPT. How about something that reflects the life of a real human child?

CHATGPT: Absolutely. Here's a grounded and emotionally rich pitch for a children's show centered on the real experiences of a child, with a focus on authenticity and emotional resonance:

Logline: Nine-year-old Nia navigates her everyday life – new friendships, growing responsibilities, big feelings, and her dreams of becoming a dancer – all while adjusting to her family's recent move to a new city…

EDS: Hold on, this is sounding very generic again. Ah, I thought this was going to be easy!

Well, good things are never that easy, as any Children's Media Yearbook editor will tell you.

ENTER: *The Yearbook*.

\*\*\*

This year's edition brings together leading thinkers and practitioners from across the field to explore the major developments impacting children's media today – from digital wellbeing and media literacy to representation and emerging technologies. You'll find thought-provoking articles, original research and case studies that offer both critical analysis and inspiring innovation.

The *Children's Media Yearbook* exists not only to document the state of the field but also to foster collaboration, encourage dialogue and advocate for media that reflects the diversity and richness of childhood itself. As you read through these pages, we hope you'll be inspired to think deeply, act boldly and contribute meaningfully to the future of children's media. And remember that we're in it together. We can't just ChatGPT it in.

*The Pancake Mayor and Ms Nozzle*

# The Children's Media Foundation: Chair's Report

**Anna Home OBE**, Chair, Children's Media Foundation

This has been a year of consolidation for the Children's Media Foundation (CMF). Our board represents a cross-section of the people and organisations concerned with achieving the best media experiences for children and young people. Dr Elizabeth Molovidov is our latest board director and we're pleased to welcome back academic representation with the return of Jeanette Steemers, professor of culture, media and creative industries at King's College London. The CMF board focuses on policy decision-making and the strategic direction of the organisation.

Meanwhile the executive group, chaired by Alison Stewart, takes on most of the everyday work of the foundation. It also increased in size and its volunteers carry out a wide range of activities and initiatives, including policy development, campaigning, regular public events, liaising with the academic research community, reaching out to the children's media industry, regular monthly newsletters and this *Yearbook*.

CMF events continue to be popular:

"Reaching kids where they are" in January 2025 was, in fact, oversubscribed! Held at Guildhall in London, it was a thought-provoking, creative and business-oriented session in which makers and channel owners on YouTube, Roblox and other social platforms explained their strategies, what generates interest and revenue and the challenges for creatives in these spaces.

"Fake news and misinformation" in April 2025 explored the issues around young people accessing and verifying news and information in an increasingly complex and manipulative environment. It considered how many young people are being negatively affected by the fake reporting and misinformation they encounter in the media they consume. Topics discussed included media literacy, fact-checking, the role of social media in social and democratic life, and how best to protect young people from mis- and disinformation while still maintaining freedom of choice. A wide range of speakers explored what is being done to help young people make their way through this minefield of misinformation. This will be an ongoing issue and has significant implications for democracy across the world.

Events are time consuming to organise, but they are valuable as we learn so much from the speakers invited and the audience's questions and concerns. They also raise the organisation's profile and sometimes even some cash – as in the case of our popular autumn QuizNite events!

Regular virtual coffee mornings and evenings are another way to reach out to the industry, academia and children's advocates, who enjoy the informal chats with the various guests. Once again CMF listens and learns.

As always executive group members will be active at this year's Children's Media Conference – producing several sessions, promoting the *Yearbook* and the work of the foundation. The executive group entirely comprises volunteers, with busy careers of their own. They are at the heart of CMF and hugely important. We owe them heartfelt thanks.

As I reported in last year's edition, the CMF-coordinated All-Party Parliamentary Group no longer exists. But we continue to have great support in parliament especially from Baroness Benjamin, and also from Baroness Kidron with her continuing concern for children's online safety and, more recently, increased involvement in AI and copyright regulation. We should also congratulate a great supporter of children and young people, the recently ennobled Baroness Longfield, previously the Children's Commissioner for England, Anne Longfield.

During the last 12 months there has been a clear and positive change in our relationship with Ofcom and the Department for Culture, Media and Sport – key parties that CMF needs to influence if we are to achieve change. Both now recognise that our long-held concerns about the future of quality children's media are 'coming home to roost'. The massive change in viewing habits amongst young people is not only an issue for children's broadcasters, but is starting to impact on the adult audience too. And the question of what happens when an audience for content viewing primarily on unregulated platforms, operated from outside the UK – how that affects young people's view of the world, and themselves, and how that affects revenues for production, and the future of effective public service regulation – are now all mainstream concerns.

> **"The crisis of childhood has become a crisis of content."**

The 'crisis of childhood' we discussed at the Children's Media Summit has become a 'crisis of content'. It's creation, it's funding and, of course – as we have said many times – it's 'finding'. The ways in which new platforms search and use recommendation systems will inevitably change people's priorities and viewing profiles is now a priority for the foundation, which we will continue to pursue with the regulator, government and the platforms themselves.

# Be Positive: This Is An Opportunity For Change

 **Colin Ward**, Research, Policy and Deputy Director, Children's Media Foundation

The Children's Media Foundation's long-running campaign to promote the value and importance of high-quality, public service media content for children has been a marathon, not a sprint. The core idea was present back in 2006, when we were called Save Kids TV and our message was perhaps a little simpler; *'Children deserve the best television'*. It was an effective message that was asking policymakers to find ways to maintain the set of standards embedded in the public service broadcaster licenses and the Ofcom code. As the sector became globalised, how could we ensure UK kids had access to a *range* of safe, quality media content – factual, entertainment, drama and animation – that reflected their own lives and the society they were growing up in. Basically, how would we stop people from serving up any old rubbish.

When you look at what has happened over the last, almost 20 years, you might be forgiven for thinking we've failed. In what has been a highly competitive environment, it is not surprising that most media businesses have prioritised commercial concerns and focused on entertainment content with a global appeal over UK-cultural content that embodies more traditional public service media values. So we have seen a steady decline in first-run, UK-originated content – particularly live action factual and drama – that is clearly age-appropriate and where the stories reflect our children's lives and communities.

Our allies in the children's production, platform and distribution sectors have fought against this decline and have never given up. The people working at BBC Children's and S4C have continued to argue the case for quality media experiences for kids and have still managed to provide the audience with some wonderful content over the years. Many commercial providers, like Sky, understand the importance of the UK family audience to their business and they also understand the ethical argument for producing life-enhancing children's media experiences. Channel 5 has continued to invest in content for younger audiences for *Milkshake!* and Channel 4 has carved out its own niche trying to reach older teen audiences. And let's not forget the excellent work of the Young Audiences Content Fund, which brought much needed additional money into the sector and supported the development of businesses and new IP that has more than repaid the government's initial investments.

Policymakers must not forget that the UK children's media production sector has the creative skills and the talent to give young people the very *best* media experiences. But the sector urgently needs a solution to two interconnected problems; funding and finding. Where will the money come from to make quality kids' content when so many platforms are offering 'free', low-quality content that does not share our public service values. And how will the audience find the high-quality content that is made for them when they are being pushed to view lower-quality content that is more easily monetised.

Those are the problems the Children's Media Foundation has been focused on over the last two years. After months of meetings with key stakeholders across the UK's children's media sector, we brought together broadcasters, industry associations and audience advocates at the Children's Media Summit 2024. The outcome of the summit was a set of policy documents we could then share with policymakers – including both the government and opposition parties – which brought together all of our shared concerns and proposed a range of solutions to tackle the 'funding and finding' problem. Those documents informed amendments to the 2024 Media Bill, which we proposed through both the Labour and LibDem parties in both Houses of Parliament, calling for deeper investigation of the significant changes in viewing by the younger audience. These were not incorporated in the Media Act, but the stage had been set and it was satisfying to hear all three major political parties praise the foundation for the long-term work put into bringing the issue to public attention.

And then… there was an election and a change of government.

The CMF had met with the new DCMS minister, Stephanie Peacock, before the election to discuss the policy proposals from the 2024 summit. We also had a good relationship with the Secretary of State, Lisa Nandy, going back to when she worked with Baroness Benjamin to set up the All-Party Parliamentary Group on Children's Media, which the CMF helped to co-ordinate. So, we asked for a meeting with the minister and eventually met with Stephanie and her team in December.

As it turned out, there was a lot happening in December. In our meeting with the minister, we emphasised the impact negative media experiences were having on children, citing the influence of Andrew Tate and the 'manosphere' on young boys, which was to become a major concern for policymakers as a result of the excellent drama series, *Adolescence*. We spoke of the urgency of the problem and the need for additional funding to support public service media content, explaining the advantages and, also, the limitations of tax relief, along with the moral case for a levy on the businesses making profits from the children's audience. We stressed the importance of Ofcom's role and asked for children's media to be at the heart of their public service review. And we asked if government could speak with all the relevant parties – platforms, PSBs, the video-sharing platforms – to ask them to work together to resolve these issues.

Then, in that fallow period between Christmas and the New Year, the *Today* programme asked Baroness Floella Benjamin, a staunch ally of the CMF and an advocate for quality children's media, to be their guest editor. The show was fascinating in many different ways, but, from a CMF perspective, the most interesting moment was the interview with Lisa Nandy, where she confirmed she had written to the video sharing platforms to ask them to consider how they could make pro-social content more prominent. She also said she had written to Ofcom to ask them to give serious consideration to the children's media experiences in their 2025 Public Service Media Review.

We followed that up in January with a meeting with Ofcom officials to find out how they were responding to the Secretary of State's request and we've had a number of meetings with them since then to talk about how we can work together to find solutions to the funding/finding problem. We have also had further meetings with DCMS officials to ask about progress and were told there had been discussions with the key stakeholders to address the government's concerns and a full report with a range of options will be shared with the ministerial team.

One of the things that was satisfying about our work this year was the feeling that we had turned a corner. Finally, after years of dogged persistence, constantly developing and refining our message, we found that we were pushing at open doors and would hear people saying many of the things that were first discussed in the CMF's multi-authored, 2021 report, *Our Children's Future: Does Public Service Media Matter*. We know our influence is limited and every individual and organisation involved in this debate has its own ideas and agenda, but we can feel confident that the CMF's campaigning work has helped to shape that debate.

For our next steps, we will be returning to the question of how we define 'quality' media experiences for children and what sort of system might be able to identify such content and ensure it is given greater prominence. Then we will be sharing those ideas with the DCMS. We will also be responding to Ofcom's Public Service Review, hoping to find practical options indicating how the government can create a regulatory framework that will improve the quality of children's media lives. And we will be asking our supporters and allies to join us for a second Children's Media Summit to discuss those proposals, which we are hoping to convene this autumn.

> **"This year is an opportunity to bring about change … this is the time to propose solutions."**

This year is an opportunity to bring about change. Everyone is now talking about what is wrong with children's media experiences, so this is the time to propose solutions. It has been a marathon but, potentially, we could be on the last mile. Let's get this done.

# Authors' Licensing and Collecting Society

Think writers should be paid for their work?

So do we.

We collect money for writers and make sure it's paid to them. Since 1977 we have paid over £700 million to writers!

Register for membership at

alcs.co.uk

ALCS is proud to support The Children's Media Foundation

# Jackanory At 60!

**Dr Diane Charlesworth**, Independent Scholar and Senior Honorary Fellow of the University of Lincoln

The first episode of *Jackanory* was broadcast 13th December 1965. From an original series envisioned to run six weeks, it went on to run for around 3,500 episodes across three decades. The programme was conceived in an era that has been described as "the second golden age of children's literature" (through the 1950s into the 1970s), with a "radical expansion and diversification of children's publishing…" (Pearson, 2013). These were the decades that saw a strong political, social and educational focus on childhood, literacy and children's literature. During the 1950s, British publishers began to establish specific children's lists and to appoint staff focused solely on working in that area, for example, Mabel George at OUP, Phillippa Pearce and then Pam Royds at André Deutsch, Judy Taylor at The Bodley Head, and Eleanor Graham followed by Kaye Webb at Puffin (Reynolds, 1998). The Children's Book Circle was founded in 1962, responsible for the awarding of the Eleanor Farjeon Award, first presented in 1965. 1965 was the year that Anne Wood established and edited the quarterly magazine *Books for Your Children*, for parents, teachers and librarians, and founded the first Children's Book Group, which became the Federation of Children's Book Groups in 1968. All this occurred in a climate of increases in government funding of school and public libraries (Reynolds, 1998; Pearson, 2016).

At the BBC, Joy Whitby who had worked in children's radio and then crossed to children's television, had placed storytelling in the preschool magazine programme *Play School* created for BBC2 in 1964. When asked to create a 15-minute teatime slot on BBC1 by Michael Peacock, newly appointed controller for the channel, Whitby looked to broaden storytelling to the 8–11-year-old audience (Whitby, 2014). Given its scheduling, she and the production team, which included Anna Home, Molly Gibbs and Angela Beeching, decided that it had to have a hook for what Whitby called the 'eavesdropping audience' of parents/adults (BBC, 2007). Good storytelling needed skilled narrators, so for this *Jackanory* teams turned to actors from the theatre, from film, and over the decades, increasingly from across television. A scan through the list of story readers via the BBC Genome database of the *Radio Times*, uncovers a roll call of artistic names across the years that includes Margaret Rutherford, Joyce Grenfell, Celia Johnson, Zia Mohyeddin, Harry H Corbett and Kenneth Williams through to Bill Paterson, Art Malik, Kathy Burke and Alexei Sayle.

Whilst the original production team had issues at the start in getting people to sign up, relatively quickly it became a badge of honour and recognition to be invited as the *Jackanory* storyteller.

The actors' union, Equity, complained to the BBC when it became known that Caroline Benn, educationalist, writer and the wife of Tony Wedgewood Benn, had done a five-part recording of *Charlotte's Web* to be broadcast in May 1966, as she was not a signed-up member of the union. The BBC defended her participation stating that "those who took part in the programme were chosen for their special ability to tell stories to children," (cited in Anon, 1966, 11). In those early days, this had included other non-actors such as Eileen Colwell, a key figure in children's library services, and Alfred William 'Bob' Roberts, a bargeman and a folksinger, who told stories of ships and the sea (Home, 1993, p. 82).

In those early years, the production team drew from the first golden era of children's literature, AA Milne, Arthur Ransome, E Nesbit, Alison Uttley, PL Travers and Richmal Crompton. There were weeks dedicated to traditional tales from countries and continents around the world – France, Italy, Switzerland, Norway, Canada, New Zealand, Japan, China, India, Africa, the Middle East – and folk stories from the different nations of Britain as well as Ireland. Northern European writers were well represented – Astrid Lindgren with her young heroine, Pippi Longstocking, Erich Kästner's capture of 1920s Berlin through children's eyes in *Emil and the Detectives*, the fairytales of Hans Christian Andersen, Tove Jansson's landscapes and characters of Moominvalley and Nils-Olof Franzén's detective, Agaton Sax.

Some authors would read their own works, for example the naturalist and conservationist, Gerald Durell, and the 14-year-old Lindsay Brown reading her novel *The Treasure of Dubarry Castle* (Triggs, 1980). Quentin Blake told stories about his character Lester whilst drawing the story illustrations live on an enormous paper-covered wall in the studio (BBC, 2007). In 1984, Charles, the then Prince of Wales, read the story that he had made up for his two younger brothers, *The Old Man of Lochnagar*. In 1996, Floella Benjamin read her story of travelling as a child from Trinidad to join her parents in London, *Coming to England* (BBC Genome Project).

Some authors had begun as BBC writers/adapters, producers or camerapersons whilst or before going on to write children's fiction – Mary Treadwell, Phillippa Pearce, Michael Bond, Jenny Nimmo and Jenifer Wayne.

In the time-honoured tradition of the Children's Television Department inviting audience participation, competitions were run for children to send in their own stories and poems, sometimes written to a theme, but on occasions left to the junior writers' interests and imagination. The first of these were broadcast in 1968 and then became a recurring feature across the 1970s and 1980s (BBC Genome).

New works were also commissioned or unpublished works given visibility. Noel Streatfeild wrote *The Barrow Lane Gang* specifically for the programme. It was read by *Likely Lads* actor, Rodney Bewes in November 1966 (BBC Genome). Joan Aitken was commissioned to write a story, and she delivered *Arabel's Raven*, a tale of the Jones family and their five-year-old daughter's pet bird, Mortimer, read in May 1971 by Roy Kinnear. More stories followed leading to a long-standing relationship between Aitken,

Quentin Blake who illustrated the stories, and Bernard Cribbens who narrated them (Beeching, 1993). The character of Little Nose, the cave boy who got into continual scrapes, appeared in stories written and illustrated by the Scotsman, John Grant. He had originally written them for his own children and up to then been unable to find a publisher for them. He read episodes from October 1969, becoming a frequent contributor to the programme, with 55 episodes to his name (BBC, 2007). In 1987, *Jackanory* joined forces with *The Guardian* and the publisher Faber in a competition for unpublished authors (Triggs 1988). The winning story, *Andi's War* set during Greece's civil war by Billi Rosen, was screened across five days in March 1988 read by Hannah Gordon.

Over the years, the *Jackanory* teams brought the child viewer Greek myths and legends, fairytales, realist and fantasy animal stories, time-slip narratives, high and low fantasy adventures, medieval tales through to narratives set during the Second World War. There were family stories, school stories, stories about orphans, children being homeless or refugees or migrants. Some stories brought controversy and criticism. The combination of Rik Mayall and Roald Dahl with the serialisation of *George's Marvellous Medicine* in 1986 generated an anarchic carnivalesque that brought numerous parent complaints (BBC, 2007). In 1992, Anna Home, as Head of Children's Television, was forced to defend the serialisation of the Australian writer Morris Gleitzman's *Two Weeks with the Queen*. A coming-of-age, but also to-realisation and to-terms story dealing with child terminal cancer, homophobia and AIDS, plans for its broadcast generated lurid headlines in the *Daily Mail*. The article quoted a Tory MP calling the project 'child abuse' and Mary Whitehouse's National Viewers and Listeners' Association's (now Media-Watch UK) complaint: "Why can't the BBC let children be children?" (Middlehurst, 1992, 5). In 1994, a late scheduling change to an earlier time slot saw parents angered by animated inserts to Ted Hughes's eco-science fiction story, *The Iron Woman* that scared young viewers (BBC, 2007).

The aesthetics of the programme changed across time, reflecting perceptions about children's engagement, attention and expectations in an increasingly media-saturated world. The original formula was "disarmingly simple" and "an experiment in TV minimalism," (BBC, 2007), a talking head directly addressing the camera and cutaways to picture illustrations. For some stories however, live action sequences were shot on location but with no dialogue, for example, Lucy M. Boston's *The Children of Green Knowe* in 1966, which was filmed at the author's own house (Homes 1993, pp. 89–90). Over time, the actors as storytellers became more mobile, often moving about the studio set that was dressed as a key place and space of the story being told and performing some of the actions of the story's main character. Tony Robinson is remembered, with director David Bell, for taking the story of *Theseus the Hero* out on location, narrating to a mobile camera, using twentieth-century slang and contemporary references, and transforming the ancient story into a form of reportage (Robinson, 1986).

The series closed its first long run on March 24th 1996, as satellite and cable brought in the first wave of new children's channels. In 2005, it was revived, not as a regular feature but in special editions pitched for the CBBC audience, the choice of texts mapping the contemporary trend in older child/young adult fiction and family film for high fantasy worlds. The format was revived for younger audiences, as *Jackanory Junior*, for two series between 2007–2009, where green screen technology enabled the storytellers to walk in the pages of the book. The programme's legacy lives on in *CBeebies Bedtime Stories* (2002–present). In 2024, the brand embraced both offline and online approaches to childhood literacy, by launching, in partnership with the Book Trust, dedicated Bedtime Stories reading corners in local libraries whilst expanding the library of past episodes available on the BBC iPlayer (BBC, 2024).

As a child of the 70s, I walked in so many different worlds and learned so many different things through this combination of the power of television and the written word. I am delighted to write this celebration of a programme, the creative and artistic synergies of which focused on instilling a love of reading in its child audience: happy anniversary, *Jackanory*!

## References

Anon (1966). "Mrs Benn answers Equity protest," *The Times*, Tuesday, May 24, p. 11.

BBC Genome Programme Index, available at https://genome.ch.bbc.co.uk/genome

BBC (2024). "Nationwide bedtime routines enhanced as CBeebies digital library is created," BBC Media Centre, February 27, available at https://www.bbc.com/mediacentre/2024/nationwide-bedtime-routines-enhanced-as-cbeebies-bedtime-stories-digital-library-is-created

BBC (2007). *The Story of Jackanory* [BBC4 documentary], available at https://www.youtube.com/watch?v=pmI1lWt7Muw

Beeching, A. (1993). "The Making of Mortimer and Arabel," *Books for Keeps*, 82, September, available at https://booksforkeeps.co.uk/article/the-making-of-mortimer-and-arabel/

Home, A. (1993). *Into the Box of Delights: A History of Children's Television*, London, BBC Books.

Middlehurst, L. (1992). "BBC accused of 'child abuse' as AIDS spreads to Jackanory," *Daily Mail*, Saturday December 12, p. 5.

Pearson, L. (2013). *The Making of Modern Children's Literature in Britain: Publishing and Criticism in the 1960s and 1970s*, London, Routledge [e-book].

Reynolds, K. (1998). "Publishing Practices and the Practicalities of Publishing," in Reynolds, K. & Tucker, N. (eds.) *Children's Book Publishing in Britain since 1945*, Ashgate Publishing Limited, pp. 20–41.

Robinson, T. (1986). "Ways of Telling," *Books for Keeps*, 40, September, available at https://booksforkeeps.co.uk/article/ways-of-telling/

Triggs, P. (1988). "Sound and Vision: *Andi's War* – a winning newcomer," *Books for Keeps*, 49, March, online at https://booksforkeeps.co.uk/article/sound-vision-march-1988/

Triggs, P. (1980). "Meet Lindsay Brown," *Books for Keeps*, 5, November, online at https://booksforkeeps.co.uk/article/meet-lindsay-brown/

Whitby, J. (2014). *Interview*, BBC Oral History Collection, available at https://connectedhistoriesofthebbc.org/play/?id=425

# I'll Tell You A Story, About Jackanory...

**Jeremy Swan**, former producer and director

*This extract, discussing his time directing Jackanory, is taken from Jeremy's Is That You, Maureen? My Life Making Children's Television & Beyond, published by Ten Acre Films and available from tenacrefilms.bigcartel.com.*

As the director of Jackanory, I had to write 15-minute scripts. Books were carved up to fill these slots – we called it 'adapting'. Once adapted you punctuated the scripts with illustrations called captions. Then you directed in the studio. The captions were a strategic device for editing the shows. If the narrator had a hiccup in the narration you just re-recorded the section in between the captions. You had to come up with a set in which to present the story. So, a set designer was on board. Then the casting, this was a doddle. Famous actors were chomping at the bit to present *Jackanory* – all they had to do was to read the autocue and display their unique talents. They had rehearsed in our offices beforehand, mainly for timing the shows.

My first show was *Witches*, presented by Rosemary Leach. I used the music of *Mars, the Bringer of War* by Holst. Anna Home, the boss, said it would scare the pants off the kids, so we switched to a bit of Tchaikovsky. From there, I nervously moved on to other shows. I loved Anna Home. She was dubious about me, but she knew that I had something to offer.

For *The Magic Pudding*, I wanted Barry Humphries to read it, dressed as a wombat. That was shot down, so another Australian, Rod McLennan presented it, with great aplomb. I worked with the great Ted Ray, who read *Thomas the Tank Engine*, long before Ringo Starr became the voice of the books on TV. Another triumph was Su Pollard, who read *Flaming Flamingos and Raging Robots* by Margaret Mahy. Su was both a flaming flamingo and raging robot – and a big hit with the kids.

Then along came Thora Hird to read *Mrs Pepperpot*. The set was a leafy tree, under which Dame Thora sat on a bench wearing her best summer frock (the presenters usually supplied their own costume) and a big wig (presenters, if necessary, wore their own wigs too). We were about to start the rehearsal of the opening episode when the control room, where I was controlling, suddenly filled up with Very Important Guests of the Director-General, wanting to see television in the making. The only television being made that morning was *Jackanory's Mrs Pepperpot*. They all hoped to see *The Onedin Line* but – that's show business.

There was a technical glitch, so we had to stop and start. Thora's opening line was: "Hello! Do you know Mrs Pepperpot? You don't? Well, she was a little woman who shrank to the size of a pepperpot at the most inconvenient moments…"

The technical hitch forced Dame Thora to keep repeating the opening lines. She was getting a bit beady. The DG's guests watched intensely – they were enjoying all the creative tension. OK. Everything fixed, we started again. The signature tune played over the kaleidoscope – 'Jackanory, Jackanory', then we dissolved to Dame Thora on the bench. The camera tracked in. Dame Thora glinted into the lens.

"Hello! Do you know Mrs Pepperpot? You don't? Well, sod *off*!"

\*\*\*

The artists who painted the pictures for *Jackanory* were a talented bunch. The Children's Graphic Department was headed by Hilary Hayton. She and Mina Martinez, Paul Birkbeck, Graham McCallum and Laurence Henry did the illustrations for *Play School* and *Jackanory*. Outside geniuses were also recruited – the likes of Quentin Blake, Jan Brychta, Gareth Floyd, Julek Heller, Jan Pieńkowski and Richard Kennedy. All wonderful artists. *Jackanory* was a tall order. At least 60 pictures were needed for each week's worth of programmes. Whatever happened to all those beautifully executed paintings? Well, I have a few. So does Anna, along with Angela Beeching, who became the show's producer. She has hundreds stashed under her spare bed.

Anna Home gave me a book to adapt – *The Land of Green Ginger* – a sort of sequel to *Aladdin* by American writer Noel Langley, originally published in 1938. He had also been a screenwriter on MGM's *The Wizard of Oz*, starring Judy Garland. If any Friends of Dorothy thought that *The Wizard of Oz* was camp, then by jingo – read *The Land of Green Ginger*! It was full of funny innuendo, strange voices and magic. But who was to perform it? Anna and I racked our brains and combed through *Spotlight*, the actors' directory.

In my bedsit in Vicarage Gate, I used to listen to *Round the Horne* on the radio – a hilarious show. The most hilarious star in it was Kenneth Williams, so perfect and right for *The Land of Green Ginger*. Anna agreed, so I rang his agent, Peter Eade, and made the offer.

Mr Eade doubted that Kenneth Williams would be interested, so I made a big pitch of how the children would love him and that Mr Williams would have a fun time, et cetera. I mentioned that I was a friend of Siobhán McKenna. Kenneth had been the Dauphan to her *Saint Joan* during the London run.

*Kenneth Williams in Jackanory*

The bait was being sniffed. It then went a bit wobbly because Hattie Jacques had fibbed to him. "You realise you have to wear a big hat that lights up with *Jackanory* in neon on the top?"

The dissuasion that followed got Kenneth to agree to do the show and enabled me to get him into a kaftan. He moaned that he looked like Beatrice Lillie. But our rocky path to the studio was evened out by Kenneth falling in love with Jonathan Cohen, who was playing the music for the episodes. Kenneth's narration was magnificent and the audience loved him – particularly when he leaned into the camera at the end of the episodes and announced emphatically, "Good-*bye!*"

Kenneth became the second-best most popular presenter on *Jackanory*. The first-best most popular presenter was Bernard Cribbins. The last *Jackanory* I directed Kenneth in was *James and the Giant Peach*. By then, he had become a dear and hilarious friend.

Another *Jackanory* hit featured Dame Judi Dench reading Beatrix Potter's *The Tailor of Gloucester*. Judi had done *Jackanory* before and had the performance technique down to a fine art. She used to get into a huddle with the autocue operator and go through the script in detail – underlining and highlighting every word. The autocue operators had to establish the closest rapport with the presenter, rolling the printed dialogue in perfect coordination with the artist's performance.

Another star who entered my galaxy through *Jackanory* was Elaine Stritch, reading *Charlie and the Great Glass Elevator* by Roald Dahl, a firm favourite author with children. Elaine had all the ingredients of a great Broadway Star: filthy temper, a drink problem, a mean-spirited disposition, and an enormous talent, living in London's Savoy Hotel with her dachshund, Bridget. Elaine's residency at The Savoy was secured by plugging the hotel on every chat show she appeared. "Before you ask me any questions, Russell (or Terry or Melvyn Bragg), let me tell you that I am living in the BEST HOTEL IN THE WORLD – The Savoy!" Well, that guaranteed free digs.

For *Jackanory*, Elaine wore a wonderful navy-blue suede trouser suit, designed by Janet Ibbotson. She told me that her fee had paid for the matching little hat that she didn't wear on camera. I doubted that she had paid for the suit. Couture exposure on TV was always a couture boost.

On the second day of us recording *Charlie and the Great Glass Elevator*, Elaine hadn't turned up when due to start. I filled in with caption rehearsals. Finally, the floor manager, Clair Dean, informed me that our star had arrived at reception.

"Tell her I'm hopping mad!" I could hear the flurry of Elaine's arrival in the studio. Then Clair told me that I was to shut my eyes in the control room. I complied and could hear a lot of shuffling, laughing and moving of cameras on the studio floor. "You are to open your eyes now, Jeremy," said Clair.

There, on the monitors, in a big close-up, was Bridget the dachshund, wearing a bandana on her head, sitting in Elaine's chair, behind which the diva herself was hiding, speaking in canine tones.

"Hi, Jeremy, Bridget here, saying I'm very sorry for delaying that naughty Elaine. I had to have a *wee-wee* in Shepherds Bush!"

# A Box Of Delights

**Richard Marson**, Writer and Producer

*Jackanory* and *Play School*… *Blue Peter* and *Record Breakers*… *John Craven's Newsround*… *Vision On*… *Grange Hill*… *Multi-Coloured Swap Shop*… *The Really Wild Show*…

…just a few titles from the long roll call of formative, influential and much-loved programmes made for successive generations of children by the BBC during an era of extraordinary creativity, captured in my forthcoming book, *A Box of Delights*. The book started life after I wrote the biography of legendary *Blue Peter* Editor Biddy Baxter. The publishers requested a follow-up, suggesting a history of British children's programmes. I told them that this was far too broad a subject for one book. I went back with a revised proposition – a history of the heyday of BBC children's programmes covering the years 1967 to 1997.

Why the choice of these particular dates?

1967 was an obvious starting point because it was then that the BBC decided to reinstate the Children's Department after several years in which its output had been asset stripped to other areas and the remainder merged within a hybrid unit called Family Programmes, incorporating another 'ghetto' area – Women's Programmes. A new boss was appointed to run the revived Children's Department – Monica Sims – and her indefatigable and inspired leadership triggered a period of great expansion and constant ambition. In 1978, Monica was succeeded by her deputy, Edward Barnes, a man with the knack of spotting gaps in the schedule and coming up with the right shows to fill them – it was his vision which led to the launch of *John Craven's Newsround*, the world's first regular news service for children and *Multi-Coloured Swap Shop*, bringing vividly to life what had been a Saturday morning TV wasteland. Following his retirement in 1986, Anna Home was appointed, with a distinguished and highly successful track record in children's drama (*Grange Hill* was launched under her watch) and returning to the BBC from a stint as an executive at the ITV company TVS. Anna remained in post until 1997, presiding over an era of rapidly increasing change – from new technology and growing competition to internal forces like the 'indie' quota and the many BBC reforms of the era, including 'Producer Choice' and the split between broadcast and production. Her departure on the eve of yet more tectonic change, felt exactly the right stopping point for the book – what followed belongs in another volume, perhaps.

Born in 1966, I was lucky not only to be a viewer during these years, but, once I'd left university, to join the BBC and, before long, the children's department, located in the unlovely confines of Television Centre's East Tower. The training I received there was constantly challenging, sometimes dispiriting, frequently euphoric – and it led to a career which continued for over three decades, during which I spent the majority of time making programmes for children – in my view the most rewarding audience for whom to work.

The period covered in the book is one of intense innovation and startling creativity (with a few notable disasters and belly flops along the way), in which there was also a deep continuity; only three Heads of Department, all of them demonstrably vocational, rather than passing through on the way to somewhere more powerful and lucrative. During this time, both the BBC and ITV ringfenced airtime for younger viewers each afternoon and at various points over the weekend. Such was the energy and commitment to this output that despite there being only three or four channels, the mix was rich, varied and continually evolving – while programme makers were guaranteed sizeable audiences. There was no means of recording or time-shifting (which could be intensely frustrating if circumstances contrived so that you missed the latest instalment of a gripping serial) but this lent television a sense of occasion and event. Each morning, the UK's playgrounds were full of chatter about what had been shown the previous afternoon.

The aim for the book is to offer more than a wallow in nostalgia. It is also a warning from history, encapsulating what can be achieved when the financial, political and public will exists to provide British children with content (not a word which was in use during the period I cover) – giving them the best tailor-made entertainment and information, reflecting the world in which they live, their rich and diverse culture and history, and aware of the nuances of catering for children of different ages.

> "It is a warning from history, encapsulating what can be achieved when the financial, political and public will exists to provide British children with … the best tailor-made entertainment and information."

Children still want to soak up knowledge and immerse themselves in fabulous and enriching stories. They continue to love animals, making things, learning about other children's lives and having the wonders and challenges of the world decoded in a way they can understand. They remain at the forefront of technological innovation – and television is now old media. Today's children are more likely to be found on their smartphones, not just consuming content, but making and sharing it via TikTok, Instagram, YouTube. These platforms will no doubt be superseded by others and few can predict the likely long-term impact of AI.

These days, there are no shortage of scandals to inflame the public but alas the steady and remorseless haemorrhaging of high-quality home-grown children's content isn't showy enough to grab the headlines and pile on the necessary pressure to effect change. Retreat and decline continue. During the interviews I conducted for the book with those who learnt their trade on children's programmes, over and again I heard the lament about all that's been lost. In many cases, these are people who have become international leaders in their field, like Anne Wood, the co-creator of *Teletubbies* and

*In the Night Garden*, who told me: "The market has completely disappeared. It's dire. It's all become ruled by money. From the 60s to the 80s, economically speaking, it was a much more buoyant time. There was also that post war feeling of making a better world, so there was more of a corporate commitment to things that might cost money and didn't have much in the way of profit, but were seen as worthwhile in themselves. Now I think it's very close to being completely dead. I used to think, 'Oh, it's only sleeping, people will realize the error of their ways and come round'. The people in power don't care. They don't have the sense of values that we had. The barbarians aren't at the gate. They're all inside it, counting their money."

The contemporary crisis in children's content is not the subject of this book, but it is a kind of subtext, a reminder that the heyday of BBC children's programmes only lasted for a relatively brief and precious period in time – which is irrevocably over.

Director Nigel Douglas cut his teeth on shows like *Grange Hill* and *The Biz!* and has a long track record in adult drama: "I remember that period in children's as being very free. You were valued and could try things out. Everything was about the show, not about anyone's ego. When I was doing children's drama, there was a producer and a director, and an associate, and the three of you ran the show. You didn't need anybody else. Years later, I went back to do *The Dumping Ground*. It had all the people we now apparently have to have to make drama. What it didn't have was any joy. Pretty much everything I did in Children's had a sense of joy. *The Dumping Ground* was a product of our new landscape, about what the focus groups said we needed to hit. The amount of care and love that we all put in all the time, in all the areas, didn't really exist anymore. It was just, here's a show that's successful. Let's hammer it."

The output of the Children's Department was so varied and wide-ranging that the biggest challenge I faced was doing justice to this without the narrative becoming one long shopping list. The text is peppered with character studies of some of the key players and illuminated by the memories of so many of those who were there at the time, like Anna Home. "I was always wanting to do something different," she says, "but then you had to find the people who wanted to do that too. As time went on, it was more difficult to take risks. On the whole, we were left alone and we just got on with it. It was a completely different world. All you can do is hope that someone will at some stage be able to go into another rebirth, because that's what it needs."

*A Box of Delights will be published this autumn by TenAcre Films.*

# Silly Matters: 50 Years Of Aardman

**Sarah Cox**, Chief Creative Director, Aardman

In 2026 Aardman reaches the ripe age of 50 and Peter Lord along with many others from those early days are still at the studio making incredible films today. It's an impressive achievement and one that could only happen because of the passion, commitment and sense of fun from everyone who has ever worked there.

This phenomenon of course goes well beyond Aardman. Our film and animation industry in the UK is fuelled by some of the most dedicated people in the world with exceptional talents who create a wonderful range of content.

So why do we do it and what makes us care so much about the quality of what we do?

In an era when technology allows forms of animated content to be made so cheaply, why do we at Aardman continue to painstakingly craft stop frame movies that take years to create, frame by precious frame, and will we still be doing this in 2076?

My 15 years (to date) with Aardman began with the most fun project I ever worked on 'The Tate Movie Project' as part of the cultural Olympiad. The brief was 'To make a movie that every child in the UK could be a part of'. We took that mission seriously and with the help of a truly innovative (and ahead of its time) interactive team led by Dan Efergan we built a website, a social network and set up workshops all over the country to gather audio and visual assets from every child who wanted to take part in the creation of an epic animated movie that was ultimately premiered in Leicester Square. The project went on to win a BAFTA and a Guinness World Record for the most individual contributions to an animated film.

The engagement and delight of the children we worked with on that project instilled a huge sense of responsibility and respect for our audience that drives me to this day. If I am honest, before that I was making work mainly to try and impress my peers. Now what absolutely matters is that what we make is good and how we define good is does it delight our audience? Does it make them laugh? Does it make them feel? Do they care about the characters? Can we twist and surprise them? And do they recognise or relate to it in a way that connects?

The thing is that doing all this is so satisfying and fun. I am convinced that there is nothing that can beat the sound of an audience laughing at a seemingly silly throwaway moment in a film that you have in whatever capacity been a part of creating. That buzz, I think, comes from experiencing a human connection. We make films to capture and share an emotion or feeling – even if that feeling is just to giggle. We ultimately put our absolute commitment in celebrating the best of what it means to be human. To be funny, to connect and to be kind.

In our most recent feature *Wallace and Gromit: Vengeance Most Fowl* we take the silly to extremes. The attention to detail that Nick Park, Merlin Crossingham, Mark Burton and the team put into every level of production to create something that works on so many levels, from absurd slapstick to emotionally heartbreaking, is impressive. The fact that it works for such a broad global audience of both adults and children and bears multiple repeated viewing is astounding. We do it because our audience deserve this level of care and perfectionism, indeed when they can smell cynicism, or a lack of passion they will turn away. There is no point making a film if it doesn't connect.

The many hours agonising over a line of dialogue or the timing of a joke, or how long we can hold the cold stare of Feathers McGraw, all pays off when our films first play to their audience and the audience responds. The whole studio, which has been employee owned since 2018 shares the pride of each successful production. This is why Peter is still coming to the studio to make films, and I hope we are lucky enough to be still somehow taking the care to make audiences laugh and care in 2076.

*Feathers McGraw in Bafta-winning Wallace & Gromit: Vengeance Most Fowl*

# Milkshake! – A Preschool Institution

**Nick Wilson**, Independent Children's Media Consultant and Creator of Milkshake!

I tumbled into Channel 5 in bizarre fashion. I was a speaker at BAFTA's Children's TV dinner and after my speech I popped off to the gents. Two overcoats appeared, one on either side of me.

"We want a word;" "We think you can help us!"

The two overcoats were in a bid for Channel 5. The deadline for submitting bids to the ITC/Ofcom was approaching rapidly, and the Consortium needed the children's programme part of their pitch building up. So they signed me up to write them a 'philosophy/strategy/practicalities' document.

Four months later Dawn Airey was on the phone. "We won. When can you start?"

Initially I was given a weekday morning slot and a two hour block on Saturday early afternoon. Our launch schedule was wide ranging from preschool to tweens. The launch of Milkshake as an umbrella brand for younger children's programmes came a few months later.

Dawn Airey wanted to replace her morning chat show *Espresso* with children's programming for the school summer holidays. So over to me!

I bundled together what programming we had and started thinking about a name. I didn't think long. We were replacing *Espresso* with a children's programme block. So what might children drink whilst mum is having coffee? Milkshakes! It was as simple as that!

Milkshake had an immediate impact equaling the Channel's average ratings and by the end of the summer exceeded them and was still growing. Milkshake was here to stay.

The brand was made all encompassing, covering our original breakfast slot, school holidays and weekend mornings. The ratings continued to improve. Gently at first, then a key acquisition accelerated the increase: *Bear in the Big Blue House*.

*Bear* was our first major hit, and whilst it was a Disney show and on Disney Channel, we made him our own with a big PR push. Bear and his puppeteer were flown over from America and filmed inserts for Milkshake sightseeing in London.

*Naomi 'Ms Milkshake!' Wilkinson*

Bear's great quality was his humour! He was parent friendly, and quite a relaxing morning watch for mums and dads. It didn't take focus groups or market research to work out that whatever you put on for children at breakfast time has to be digestible for a grumpy dad, a harassed mum and a bored older sibling. Common sense tells you that, and I've always preferred common sense to research.

It's quite ironic that Milkshake's first burst of popularity came from an American show. As the block progressed, we branded ourselves increasingly UK-produced, and UK voices – to differentiate us from the growing tide of Disney, Viacom and Turner channels. As our US licenses came to an end, they were replaced by a raft of UK-led animation co-productions and fully funded "live" action commissions.

It was a golden period for Milkshake – everything seemed to work! Over a two to three-year period beginning in 2003/4, we commissioned, co-produced and broadcast *Peppa Pig*, *Fifi and the Flowertots*, *The Little Princess*, *Noddy* and the *Mr Men*. We also acquired, adapted and revoiced *Mia Moa* from Italy, *The Save Ums* from Canada, later *Bananas in Pajamas* and *Bottletop Bill* from Australia. We raided libraries and licensed classic series like *Rupert the Bear*, *Fireman Sam* and *Roobarb*.

To complement the animations, I commissioned documentaries for preschoolers: *School* set in a reception class, followed by *Family* shot throughout the UK, and *Animal Antics*. The ratings just carried on growing!

Our audiences equalled and sometimes surpassed CBeebies, and we were miles ahead of Nick Jr., Cartoonita and Disney Junior. It was a hugely enjoyable period! *Peppa Pig* clearly played a big part in building our audience, and the deal added revenue as well. The production company Astley Baker Davis – Neville, Mark and Phil – were located just behind Channel 5. Phil was the money, business, ducking and diving end of the team, Neville and Mark the creatives. While Mark and Neville were building Peppa's world, Phil was seeking the money to make the series and the right broadcast platform on which to launch it.

Phil had a particular style to his work: it began wide-eyed and innocent. "I've never done a deal like this before!" Followed by an amiable saunter towards the deal he really wanted. First, he cosied up with Rubber Duck (finance, production and distribution), persuading them to part-fund the series, then hit the road with their distribution executive Joan Lofts, to find a Broadcast platform.

Phil's job was made easy by the remarkable and totally engaging short pilot put together by Nev and Mark. Phil and Joan took it to the BBC, who decided they needed to think about it, so then they came to me! I didn't need to think about it. I jumped in with both feet and set about wrestling an 'acceptable' deal from the 'innocent' Phil.

We committed to a large number of episodes over several years linked to a share of secondary revenues. When the deal went before 5's legal beagles, they recommended I turn it down. Too long a commitment – what if the show flopped? I listened carefully and did the deal anyway.

It was exclusive on free-to-air but left the door open for Phil to do a deal with pay channel Nickelodeon. And with those two deals in place, they went into production. The rest is a history that leaves me with a warm glow, Peppa was an instant hit. The legal beagles now applauded my deal, and so did the C5 accountants two and half years later when Phil personally brought the first cheque representing our share of secondary revenues.

Subsequently, that deal has brought in thousands of pounds to C5, whilst 20 years on, Peppa still dominates the Milkshake schedule with three–six episodes every day. I am proud of playing a small but vital part in the start of what has become a preschool phenomenon.

By now Milkshake was firmly established as a preschool brand. Commercial success gave us the wherewithal to continue commissioning: *Roary the Racing Car*, *Hana's Helpline*, *The Beeps* and a raft of live-action shows followed.

What held Milkshake together and made it a sustained success were the presenters. From its very earliest days, Milkshake had brilliant presenters. The C5 transmission suite had a mini voice-over studio attached, and with a bit of persuasion, the powers that be added a camera. I hired Konnie Huq and Lucy Alexander to host live continuity. Both did a good, solid job, but neither stayed, with Konnie off to *Blue Peter* and Lucy into property shows.

Then kappow! I auditioned, screen tested and discovered the amazing 'Ms Milkshake!' Naomi Wilkinson. She was joined by the multi-talented Eddie Matthews who we tempted away from Nickelodeon. They were an incredible pairing and once they were joined by Kemi Majeks the backbone of the first evolution of Milkshake was born. The presenters worked full time and with their presenter's assistants prepared all of their own material and invented the blobby board – a makeshift chunk of scenery with a blob to show where to put cards and pictures so the remote camera would find them!

Naomi, Eddie and Kemi built the Milkshake direct "I'm talking to just you" style of presenting that I wanted. With live continuity seven days a week and a slowly evolving repertoire of in house productions we needed to recruit. Next to join the team was Beth Evans. She slipped into Milkshake like she had been born to it. She struck up a great friendship with Naomi and working together they made Milkshake continuity blissfully smooth and trouble-free, the perfect example of good casting – stress-free production. Of course, it was never entirely stress-free, because it was 'live'. Things would break, timings would change, and guests wouldn't turn up, but overall, I had a really easy ride as the executive in charge. Trust people to do their job, and invariably, they do.

Then came Jen Pringle. Another trained dancer and singer and her greatest asset – she came from Scunthorpe. Every channel should have a face from Scunny on the screen. Jen was fresh out of college and very young when we hired her. She was a raw, energetic talent whose enthusiasm and energy were infectious.

Once you've got a Scunny, what else do you need? A touch of the Irish... enter Derek! No children's TV experience, but a very engaging personality, and he had a delightful dog. He made an immediate impact: warm, charming, empathetic and fun. Some 15–20 years later Kemi, Derek and Jen are still to be seen on Milkshake.

*Nick Wilson's book When Will You Get a Proper Job? is available now.*

# 30 Years Of Sony PlayStation: A Revolution In Play And Youth Culture

**Dr Carla Sousa**, Assistant Professor, Lusófona University, CICANT (Lisbon, Portugal) and **Ivan Barroso**, Assistant Professor, Lusófona University, CICANT (Lisbon, Portugal)

In December 1994, a grey box entered the Japanese market that would redefine digital play for generations. Less than a year later, on the 29th of September 1995, Sony's original PlayStation, launched in Europe – and with it, so did the idea that gaming was no longer a niche pastime or child's toy, but a mainstream cultural force (Crookes, 2023). The PlayStation wasn't just another console; it was a symbol of technological confidence, marketing savvy, and – as time passed – it proved itself as a redefinition of childhood and youth culture.

This chapter briefly traces the PlayStation's 30-year history through three lenses: its impact on the gaming industry, its role in shaping children's and adolescents' cognitive and emotional development, and its influence on contemporary youth identities. For parents and educators living in a landscape in which gaming is not only ubiquitous but often misunderstood, the PlayStation's story offers both reassurance and challenge: it is the story of how play became more complex, more social, more immersive – and ultimately more powerful, with all the opportunities and challenges this brings.

## PlayStation changes the game

Before the PlayStation, gaming was largely dominated by Nintendo and Sega – companies whose design philosophy emphasised family-friendly fun, bright aesthetics and tightly controlled ecosystems. Sony, by contrast, brought a new tone. The original PlayStation embraced cinematic storytelling, 3D graphics and a disc-based format that dramatically increased storage capacity compared to cartridges. With that came music, full-motion video, and a shift toward older audiences. In fact, Sony marketed the PlayStation not as a children's toy, but as an adult-driven lifestyle object (see figure 1), like the Sony's Walkman or Discman that had come before it. This marked a fundamental shift in the view society had of console gaming for young adults and adults.

*Figure 1. Advertisement from Sony PlayStation (1995)*

By the early 2000s, the PlayStation 2 (2000) had become the best-selling console of all time, reinforced by a vast library of games and its additional functionality as a DVD player, which helped it reach even into non-gaming households. This 'Trojan horse' approach embedded gaming into everyday domestic life. Children no longer had to negotiate for 'game time'; instead, the PlayStation became part of the living room media ecology.

For developers, the PlayStation era represented new creative possibilities. Titles like *Final Fantasy VII*, *Metal Gear Solid*, and *Gran Turismo* pushed narrative, design and simulation beyond arcade-style reflexes into lands of cinematic immersion and emotional complexity. It also offered a safe and behaviourally driven control scheme that tended to better engage individuals in the game experience (Limperos et al, 2011). The console also helped in a new economics of development: cheaper production costs for discs opened doors for experimental and niche games to thrive alongside blockbusters – a trend that would only deepen with the PlayStation 3's digital marketplace and indie game ecosystem.

## Gaming, development and digital literacies

Much of the early concern around gaming and child development focused on violence and screen time (Markey and Ferguson, 2017). But across its three decades, the PlayStation platform has played a more nuanced role in shaping young people's cognitive and emotional skills. While concerns remain valid – especially around problematic content and addictive play patterns – the developmental picture is richer than early moral panics allowed (Kelly et al, 2021).

From a motor-skill perspective, action and sports games on PlayStation consoles have long been associated with improved hand-eye coordination, spatial awareness and reaction time (Rico et al, 2025). Puzzle games like *Tetris Effect* or strategy-based titles such as *Civilization VI* promote planning, memory and logical thinking. Meanwhile, role-playing games (RPGs) encourage systems thinking and decision-making, often across hours of complex gameplay.

Crucially, games on the PlayStation have grown to include deep narratives that require emotional investment. In titles like *The Last of Us* or *Journey*, players are not only solving problems, but exploring loss, grief, companionship and resilience. These emotionally resonant experiences – far from being passive – ask children and young people to navigate ethical dilemmas and form empathic responses to characters unlike themselves.

This has implications for 'digital literacies' – generally seen as the ability to make sense of and engage with complex multimedia environments (Knobel and Lankshear, 2006). Games often require reading, interpreting symbols, understanding cause-and-effect relationships and working collaboratively. In an era where media fluency is as critical as traditional literacy, games like those on the PlayStation platform offer a fertile, engaging, yet informal, pedagogical curriculum (Portier-Charneau and Sanchiz, 2024).

## Youth culture and community

Perhaps more than any other console, PlayStation has been instrumental in the mainstreaming of 'gamer' as an identity category. Its rise paralleled the transformation of gaming from a solitary hobby to a social and cultural practice. With the arrival of online functionality in the PlayStation 2 era and the PlayStation Network in 2006, gaming became increasingly community oriented.

For adolescents, this shift was profound. Gaming moved from bedrooms to networked spaces, where friendships were built, identities performed and new forms of social capital emerged (Tseng et al, 2015). Online gaming communities, streaming and esports competitions have since become integral parts of youth culture – and the PlayStation ecosystem has been central to that transformation.

PlayStation has often positioned itself at the intersection of gaming and other media. From its early support of music CD playback to contemporary tie-ins with streaming platforms, the console has helped young people navigate a hybrid media environment where boundaries between watching, playing and chatting are increasingly blurred. PlayStation games have both reflected and challenged dominant narratives around gender, race and belonging, both reinforcing and questioning prejudices through its meaning-making potential – figures 2 and 3 represent one of the potential thousands of examples of that.

For educators and parents, this has meant recognising PlayStation is more than a device: it's a cultural touchstone. Children and teens use games to express identity, to learn social norms, to experiment with rules and boundaries. To ignore this, or to see it only partially, is to risk misunderstanding the richness of their inner and social lives.

## From living room to life

As the PlayStation enters its fourth decade, it has left a massive mark, not just on the entertainment industry, but on how we think about children's play, learning and identity. In 1995, it was hard to imagine a console that would influence the aesthetics of cinema, the dynamics of friendship, the politics of representation and the psychology of emotion – even motivating fashion brands, movies or TV series. And yet, here we are.

PlayStation's success – and controversy – rests on its hybridity and duality. It is both escapist and expressive, both entertainment and education, both solitary and social – to a point it is almost paradoxical. That is why it has

*Figures 2 and 3. Evolution of the representation of Lara Croft, from Tomb Raider II (1997) to Rise of the Tomb Raider (2015).*

© Sony, Eidos Interactive, Microsoft Studios and Square Enix captivated young players for 30 years, and why it continues to shape the media landscape for those same players and their descendants.

For those of us belonging to the PlayStation generation, and in charge of educating a new one, probably the biggest task is to find the balance between those paradoxes, not demonising or glorifying it specifically, or games in general, fostering critical engagement with such an immersive media. It is also relevant to say that thinking critically about it also requires understanding and calling out Sony, the game studios and developers for their responsibility to create healthy, non-inherently addictive, inclusive and accessible gaming environments: shifting from the idea that players have all the responsibility and, consequently, all the faults. Moreover, this implies fostering technical literacies and related-knowledge in players, especially the younger ones, since if we understand how something works – including its business models – we will be able to consciously protect ourselves.

In the end, understanding the PlayStation 30-year legacy means not just reflecting on how it shaped us, but actively shaping what comes next; by raising a generation of players, educators, and creators who can enjoy games with insight, demand better from those who make them and reimagine play as a space for both joy and justice.

## References

Crookes, D. (2023). 'Sony's Game-Changer'. In Sleep, D, *The History of Video Games*, pp. 82–85. Future Publishing Limited.

Kelly, S, Magor, T. and Wright, A. (2021). 'The Pros and Cons of Online Competitive Gaming: An Evidence-Based Approach to Assessing Young Players' Well-Being'. *Frontiers in Psychology*, 12.

Knobel, M. and Lankshear, C. (2006). 'Digital Literacy and Digital Literacies: Policy, Pedagogy and Research Considerations for Education'. *Nordic Journal of Digital Literacy*, 1(1), pp. 12–24.

Limperos, AM, Schmierbach, MG, Kegerise, AD. and Dardis, FE. (2011). 'Gaming across different Consoles: Exploring the influence of control scheme on Game-Player enjoyment'. *Cyberpsychology Behavior and Social Networking*, 14(6), pp. 345–350.

Markey, P.M. and Ferguson, CJ. (2017). 'Teaching Us to Fear: The Violent Video Game Moral Panic and The Politics of Game Research'. *American journal of play*, 10(1), pp. 99–115.

Portier-Charneau, C. and Sanchiz, M. (2024). 'Effects of the instructional message used to introduce game-based learning, prior knowledge, prior gaming experience and flow on learning'. *Information and Learning Sciences*, 125(11/12), pp. 943–965.

Rico, JLC, Villarrasa-Sapiña, I, García-Massó, X. and Monfort-Torres, G. (2024). 'Differences in hand acceleration and digital reaction time between different skill levels of Counter Strike players'. *Entertainment Computing*, 52, 100797.

Tseng, F, Huang, H. and Teng, C. (2015). 'How do online game communities retain gamers? social presence and social capital perspectives'. *Journal of Computer-Mediated Communication*, 20(6), pp. 601–614.

# The Legacy Of Mary Field

**Anna Home OBE**, Chair, Children's Media Foundation

*This article first appeared in Film Review. The following article is a reproduction of Mary Field's own review of Tom's Ride from the early 1950s.*

Many adults in the UK still have fond memories of the Children's Film Foundation (CFF) films. The foundation was the first organisation in the UK to make films specifically for children, films which were geared to them reflecting their needs and interests. Mary Field, a female pioneer adult documentary maker was appointed Chief Executive of Children's Entertainment Films (CEF) by J Arthur Rank, the head of Gaumont-British Pictures, who believed that films for children could provide education and promote moral values. Many in the film world did not agree with this, believing there was little value in the children's audience (an attitude which can still apply from time to time today).

Mary Field was delighted to accept the challenge and the CEF was born. The first film which appeared in 1944 was *Tom's Ride*, a slightly heavy handed morality tale with Stewart Rome as Tom's father. Despite this, it was a great success with the target audience and the public. Mary Field was able to go ahead. She spent a great deal of her time observing how audiences reacted to the films and adjusting the content accordingly. Mary believed that children deserved good quality, professionally made films, which should be entertaining as well as educational and should reflect their own lives, interests and concerns. Over the years the films tended to become more entertaining, but always with basically moral values. These are principles which have underpinned all the organisations which have succeeded CEF, which developed into the CFF in 1951, where Mary continued her work until 1956.

The CEF/CFF was initially well funded by the Eady Levy, a tax on cinema box office receipts; the organisation received £60,000 providing enough income to fund around six

*Mary Field (centre) with Sir Edward Salisbury and Winifred Cullis.*

55-minute films a year. The films were shown in a variety of cinemas at regular Saturday morning matinees. A wide range of directors were involved, some well-established, some quite new. Probably the most famous were Michael Powell and Emeric Pressburger who collaborated on their last film together, *The Boy Who Turned Yellow* in 1972. Some directors made several films over the years, for example Harley Cokeliss, director of *The Glitterball*, and *The Battle of Billy's Pond*, and much later on *An Angel for May*. Many well known British actors started their careers in CFF films, such as Michael Crawford.

The foundation flourished until the 1980s, but the Saturday audiences gradually declined and in 1985 the Eady Levy was abolished and the foundation began to struggle. It was apparent that it was going to be increasingly difficult to fund children's films and although a few were produced in the next few years, television was becoming dominant in children's entertainment and despite the introduction of a development fund for 'family friendly films' between the UK film council and the BBC, the Board agreed that the time had come to move into the expanding world of children's TV, and so we became the Children's Film and Television Foundation (CFTF), concentrating on development. Some films were successfully developed including *Danny the Champion of the World*, a film made for TV, and a number of TV series including *The Magician's House* (1999) and *An Angel for May* (2002).

However it became clear that at this point there was little or no future in pursuing funding for traditional children's films, and around the same time it was apparent that children's TV itself was under great pressure, again there were big problems funding original content. In 2006, a campaign 'Save Kids TV' was launched. The campaign made some progress, but it became obvious that some kind of new organisation was needed to coordinate the problems going forward. It was time for another new start. In 2012 the Children's Media Foundation (CMF) began. We are no longer a development or production organisation but one which is dedicated to ensuring that children's media needs are prioritised (surely something Mary Field would have applauded). We advocate for the best possible media experiences on all platforms for young people of all ages. We have become an organisation which lobbies to ensure this policy is activated. This involves a much greater involvement in media politics. There has been much discussion in parliament about a new Media Bill, now an Act, involving the role of regulation in terms of properly funded content for children and young people, together with their safety online. We will fight to ensure that children are taken seriously.

We live in a completely different world from that of Mary Field, but her principles remain firmly in our minds. Kids deserve the best. Sadly, these days there are fewer new children's films – apart from major animated features – and also much less live-action children's TV drama. Money is tight – does that sound familiar? However there are still children's films to be seen in the UK. The BFI are currently issuing a series of collections of CFF films, including many old favourites still enjoyed by today's audiences. As the Chair of the CMF, I believe that we have an ongoing duty to follow Mary Fields guiding principles to provide content which will entertain and inspire children and young people as they grow up in an ever changing, challenging media world.

# Tom Rides On: A Review

**Mary Field CBE**, Director and Producer, 1896–1968

*Originally published in the 1950–1951 Film Review annual.*

When Mr Rank decided, in 1944, to produce some special films to do children good, he probably expected that any results of this pioneering move would be in the realm of moral education rather than in the film world. The first film to be produced under this scheme, *Tom's Ride*, when it was completed early in 1945, certainly attracted no more interest than a speck of dust falling in the troubled pond of Wardour Street. A one-reel film, dealing with the searchings of conscience of a small boy who finds a note case and finally returns it to its owner, in time for her to catch her train to see her invalid son, is strongly reminiscent of that popular early Victorian work – *Ministering Children*. No one connected with its making was particularly satisfied with it. Certainly no one expected that the audiences in the Saturday morning cinema clubs of the Gaumont and Odeon circuits, where it was shown, would receive it, not with hostility, not with indifference but with enthusiasm. The showing of *Tom's Ride* started something new in filmgoing – it provided children's audiences with a film of their own, entertainment that was not just a leftover from the adult cinema.

For the next twelve months the group deputed by Mr Rank to make the children's films – Children's Entertainment Films, CEF for short – worked away trying different kinds of short films that would put a moral before children's audiences. *Sports' Day*, a film against cruelty to animals, which by the way, launched a new artiste, Jean Simmons; a black and white cartoon; a nature film with its commentary in rhymed couplets; a sort of children's pictorial, called *Our Magazine*. These contributions to club programmes were lapped up so eagerly by club members, that CEF rashly decided to show its work to film critics and educationists. The result was not fortunate. No adults were either edified or amused. CEF retired to consider both why children liked the pictures and why their reception by grown-ups was so unkind. This period of heart-searching was of the greatest value, for it led to the great clearing of the decks for action – with Mr Rank benevolently observing and never interfering.

First, CEF sought definite terms of reference. The vague description of its films as "to do the children good" had to be clarified. The great educationist, Michael Sadler, early in the century, indicated that, while moral instruction is the work of home, church and school, indirect moral education is made up of all our contacts with life and one of the most potent factors in moral education is good example. CEF decided that children's cinema clubs of several hundred members, all having paid sixpence to enjoy themselves, was no audience for moral instruction, but would be particularly susceptible to contact with good example – so long as the goodness was not obtrusive. This then would be the job of CEF But already it was clear that the good example of a children's entertainment film was frighteningly strong. In one West Country town the children who had enjoyed *Tom's Ride* were so impressed with the hero's returning of the note-case to its rightful owner that, for at least four weeks, they brought to the cinema manager everything they picked up in the streets, until he wished Tom had never started on his famous ride!

*A still from **Tom's Ride**, with Colin Simpson as Tom and Angela Glynne as Tom's sister.*

Already there had been called in being an Advisory Council on Children's Entertainment Films, representing Government Departments and most national bodies interested in the leisure-time activities of children. It was now obvious that the closest relations between CEF and the Advisory Council must be developed if children's entertainment films and their great influence were to be developed wisely and the children subjected to the influence of no special group, religious, political or economic. Both sides, appreciating this need for collaboration, worked closely together on the script and production of the three-reeler *Jean's Plan*. Submitted to the censor, it was returned with an 'adults only' certificate and needed drastic cutting to get it approved for children's audiences. This unfortunate contretemps drew the Advisory Council and CEF closely together and, during the last five years, they have, in great amity, jointly explored the problems of their task. Throughout this period they have carried out careful research into the reactions of their juvenile audiences. With the Gaumont and Odeon Cinema Clubs available for observation, the staff of CEF has been able to study its audiences personally, all over Britain, has received detailed reports from well-briefed managers and inaugurated two new ways of testing audience reaction. One is the recording the sounds from the auditorium, where a children's audience is gloriously vocal, and favouring the sound track of the film so that one can tell which action provokes which sound; and the other, photographing one section of the audience at various points during the film by infra-red photography so that they are unconscious that they are under observation. These two innovations have been hailed by psychologists as the only sound bases for the study of audience reaction and this research is now spreading outside Britain to the Dominions and some European countries.

The care and trouble involved by this work has more than justified itself, for, out of 161 CEF productions, long stories, short stories, serials, shorts and cartoons only one has not been successful and the reason for this failure has been ferreted out and duly acted on. The innate conservatism of the audience has been noted and taken into consideration. Changes are introduced gradually but it has been found that, with caution, audiences can be accustomed to almost any kind of film so long as it is good cinema, well made with a reasonable wellknit plot. Child audiences are, on the whole, not interested in adults; they prefer, naturally enough, to see children, and ordinary children at that, like themselves. They are immensely curious and enjoy acquiring knowledge so long as they do not believe they are being instructed. The most interesting thing is that, with a few natural modifications, these rules apply to juvenile audiences all over the world.

Before the war, Russia had started making children's films primarily for its own children but, since the war, the lead in this field has been taken by the British group which is blatantly international in its outlook. It has produced its own films in fourteen different countries and stimulated other nations, especially Sweden and France, to follow its example in producing for children. The children's film movement in Czechoslovakia partly stems from a British display in 1947. CEF films show in many countries – the most successful in thirty-four – and several interesting techniques of production from an international standpoint have already been inaugurated by its staff. Partly as a result of CEF agitation, for its meeting at Florence in May, 1950, Unesco commissioned a special report on this new kind of film – the Children's Film.

For children's films are new. They fit into no known category: feature film, documentary or educational. They refuse to conform to the set regulations of exhibitors, distributors, customs officials and those who frame international agreements. A children's film frequently refuses to remain a children's film. Where there are children there is usually a family and the junior members want Mum and Dad, Papa and Mama, to see 'our' films; and when the grown-ups see a children's film they enjoy it very often more than ordinary commercial films. They, too, like to ride with Tom.

This spring CEF held its second press show to London critics, remembering the first premature airing of its wares. "Unfair to adults," cried one critic, finding these films were intended for children only. "The best entertainment I've seen for weeks," wrote another. Not a hostile voice was raised. Not a critic resented the indirect moral education, still inherent but now skilfully handled. This spring, the Scandinavian countries sent for a CEF envoy to help them develop children's films and dubs; this spring Indonesia hailed children's films with enthusiasm; this spring the USA, last perhaps of all the great countries to join this new movement, agreed with Mr Rank to show his films at Chicago in the autumn.

*Tom's Ride* is already in the National Film Archives as the first children's film, but where will *Tom's Ride* take us? All over the world, breaking up stereotyped trade conventions, breaking up established programmes, upsetting audiences and international trade agreements, taking us, perhaps, at a glorious breakneck pace to something new and international in the film world-at long last?

Proudly Supports The Children's Media Yearbook

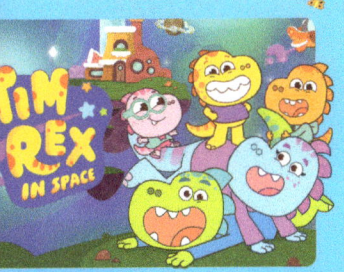

*it's all on* **5**
Watch | Stream

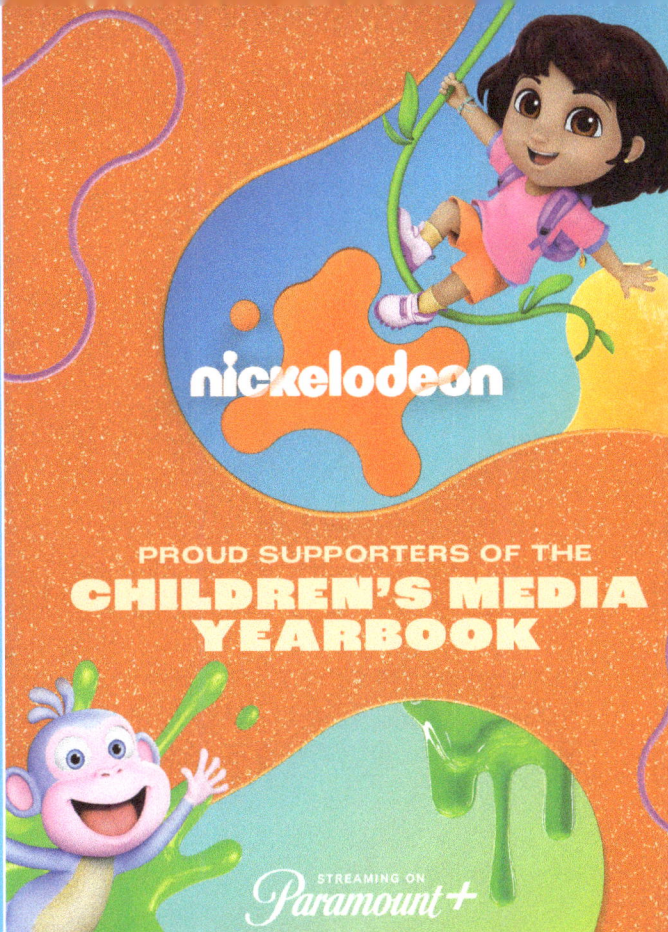

# boomkids

**BOOM KIDS** has over 15 years of experience in creating **bold** and **dynamic** content that fuels the **imagination** of preschoolers and children.

Driven by **passion** and **purpose**, we are a powerhouse of **creativity** and committed to delighting young audiences.

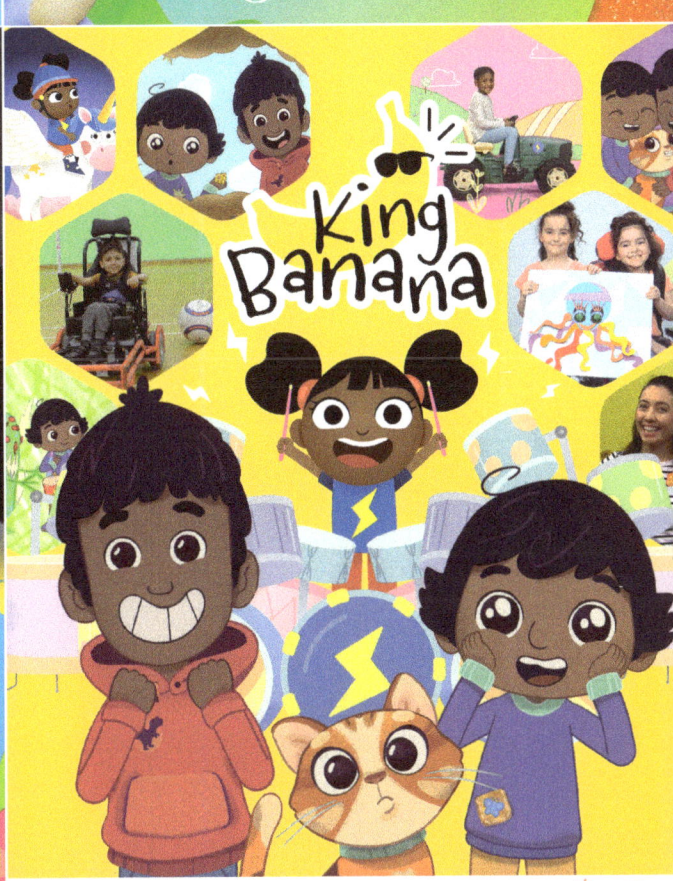

kingbananatv.com

# 'Linear TV is Dead?' Or: How I Learned To Stop Worrying And Love YouTube

**Colin Ward**, Producer, and Research, Policy and Deputy Director of CMF

So, just to be clear, that *Dr Strangelove* reference in the title does not imply that the irresistible rise of YouTube is in *any* way equivalent to the development of the nuclear bomb. That would be very silly.

Yes, you could argue that YouTube represents an existential threat to traditional children's linear platforms and the producers that create content for them. And yes, some of the stories we see in the press – such as YouTube's Youth Digital Wellbeing Initiative to promote a 'unified vision for the development of high quality, age-appropriate content for young people' – has just the faint echo of a Kubrickian dystopia, where saying something is true, makes it true. But that's as far as it goes in terms of similarities between the rise of YouTube and a 1960's film about a crazy alpha-male taking control of a weapon of mass destruction. After all, YouTube did ban Andrew Tate.

No. I chose that reference because *Dr Strangelove* was Kubrick's response to events that seemed overwhelming. And the challenges children's media creatives are facing can sometimes feel overwhelming. You have an idea for a show, but there is so little money out there it's hard to see how you can develop or produce your idea. Sure, if it's an idea for an animation for younger kids, then maybe your chances are a *little* better, although the competition is still fierce. Of course, if the animation style is very simple and there's no dialogue, then ok, maybe we can schedule a meeting. And if you think you can use AI to cut your writing and animation team to the bone, then come on up to the front of the queue and we can talk about toy deals.

It's not that it's impossible to carve out a career in live action factual, entertainment and drama for children, it's just that over the last few years it's got an awful lot harder. And let's be honest, it was never easy in the first place.

But the dark always comes before the dawn. Working together, we are going to find ways to adapt and survive. We have to. The audience *needs* people like us producing children's media content, so we will keep fighting for what we believe in. And there is definitely light on the horizon. As it turns out, YouTube wants exactly the same thing; high quality, age-appropriate and *entertaining* content that helps children to grow and learn and feel part of a community. YouTube has publicly acknowledged its responsibilities to the audience, so now it's up to us to talk to policy makers about how Ofcom, as the media regulator, can hold YouTube to its stated goals.

To understand how we might achieve that, it's important to remember how we got to this place. So, here's a quick history lesson – and feel free to skip ahead if you've heard this all before.

The commercial market for high-quality, UK-cultural kids' media content was always fragile. ITV never made any money from children's content and around 20 years ago things started to implode. Pretty soon the BBC, Sky and Five were, more or less, the only gigs in town, but they were all under financial pressure. As a result, producers became increasingly reliant on co-production finance to make budgets work, which meant a gradual move away from UK-cultural content towards either mid-Atlantic storytelling or stories selling a particular version of the UK; think Big Ben, Sherlock Holmes, posh kids and Guardsmen in bearskin hats.

About the same time, we saw the arrival of connected devices, which opened the door – or, possibly, the Pandora's box – to let the global media giants into every waking moment of a child's life. The video sharing platforms (VSPs), such as YouTube and TikTok, rode in on the crest of that wave.

So, that takes us back to that question; why should we learn to stop worrying and love YouTube? Well, maybe we can't completely stop worrying, but here's the thing that no one can or should ignore; kids *love* YouTube. And that's why we need to learn to love it as well. A bit like when one of your kids brings home a noisy and excitable new friend, but you can tell that they've bonded over a shared love of games/pranks/make-up/rabbits (delete as applicable). So, you pivot, adapt and make them welcome.

Like most people, I love YouTube because it has fantastic content for everyone. You can find almost anything, whether that's a clip from a show or some information you need. For me, YouTube offers… And let's stop there for a moment. I've just been on my account to see what the algorithm was offering and lost 10 minutes watching Paul Whitehouse talking about David Bowie on the *Graham Norton Show*; a perfect intersection of three of my favourite things!

And there is the dilemma in a nutshell; the *Graham Norton Show* is funded out of the BBC licence fee. Most children's producers would say that YouTube is happy to give the audience access to the content they love, provided the platform doesn't have to pay the going rate for producing that content. Their argument is that YouTube wants the cake for free and it will eat every crumb until there is nothing left. Of course, YouTube would argue they are just a platform offering creators the opportunity to share their content with the audience.

The problem is that it's not just a platform; it is now *the* platform. YouTube dominates children's media experiences. It offers them exactly what they want; everything, everywhere, all at once and for free! Yes, there's an important debate to be had around whether or not that is a good thing. The government might still decide to limit children's access to media content; those proposals to restrict smart phones to over-16s haven't gone away. But the reality is that YouTube has got the eyeballs, because they give kids total control over their media experiences. Children can usually find what they want to watch, and when they are tired of it, they can switch, instantaneously, to something new.

So where does traditional linear TV fit into that world? Well, a lot of people would argue that it doesn't. If you want to grab attention for your podcast or LinkedIn post then just announce that TV is dead. From that standpoint, the most recent 'appointment to view' content – such as *Gladiators* and *Love Island* – are just the final twitches of a massive beast breathing its last. But if that's true, it is describing the end of a type of delivery platform; it does not *necessarily* signal the end of TV-style media content. The real problem we face is, how do we replace the TV funding model?

To be provocative, does it matter if CBBC disappears? Or even CBeebies? What matters is the content. Children who are growing up now are entitled to the same range of culturally relevant, trusted and life-affirming content that was made available to previous generations, in a form and on platforms that reflect the way children and young people live today. The kicker is, how do we ensure that this content will be funded and how can we make sure audiences will find that content. And that is what we will be discussing at the Children's Media Conference and at the second Children's Media Summit in the autumn.

There is light on the horizon. The government understands there is a problem and they understand that children's media experiences have a far-reaching impact on their development. Yes, politicians are reluctant to intervene in the market, but they may be ready to offer some form of support, if we can present practical suggestions for a new children's media ecology that works for everyone; platforms, legacy media producers and YouTube content creators. Although, above all else, the urgent requirement is that we come up with a way of creating and sharing children's media content that works for the audience.

# TVs With Wings And Other Creatures: Imagining The Future Of TV

**Dr Cassie Brummitt**, Assistant Professor in Film and Television and **Dr Elizabeth Evans**, Professor of Screen Cultures, Institute for Screen Industries Research, University of Nottingham

The *Radio Times* commissioned research from us into how children imagined the future of television. We ran three workshops with a total of 70 children aged six to 17 where we asked them to use a range of creative media, including LEGO, Playdough and drawing, to explore what television means to them and how they imagine they will watch it in the future. This resulted in three key findings: television remains important to children, children have concerns about the future of television and children want to control their television futures.

## 1: Television remains important to children

Children understand 'television' to mean several different kinds of service including broadcast, subscription VODs and online video platforms such as YouTube. They all value watching television with family, with the home and the television set as the preferred location and technology. Children enjoy television programmes' emotional storytelling and praise them for offering a way to relax and escape when tired or anxious.

"When I come home from school, I'm so tired I just like to jump on my sofa and chill out watching telly."
6–8-year-old, male

Television is also important in helping children relate to others. In addition to regularly watching and enjoying TV with family, they frequently talk to friends about recently-aired programming – both broadcast and streaming – as a means of reaffirming social bonds.

Figure 1. A communal TV set that flies to different houses in the community (6–8-year-old, male)

When imagining future TV devices, younger children in particular frequently designed sets that encourage shared TV-watching (figure 1). Television remains part of young people's social fabric, and regularly watching streaming and broadcast content is a transgenerational and communal activity.

Television – including linear television – remains a vital part of children's cultural lives, offering them something they can share with friends and family.

## 2: Children have concerns about the future of television

When asked to imagine future television devices, children expressed uncertainty and concern regarding future media technologies and TV viewing habits. These concerns manifested in different ways depending on age group, with younger children seeking to mask concerns by making television 'friendly' and older children more openly accepting their technophobia.

Younger children (6–10-year-olds) commonly imagined television objects with anthropomorphic traits, for example by giving their devices arms, wings or faces (figure 2; figure 4). These objects were often able to interact with the user in ways that felt authentically human. Incorporating these human or natural features renders the TV more familiar, trustworthy and relatable. One group even invented a television set that would provide friendly, helpful advice and guidance, encouraging users to "get fresh air while you're watching TV" (9–12-year-old, male).

Older children (13–17-year-olds) rarely produced future devices resembling the

*Figure 2. TV with wings (6–8-year-old, male)*

traditional TV set, instead imagining objects that were intensely technological and futuristic. These devices drew on science-fiction dystopian imagery, featuring technological augments that invade or control the body such as microchips, surgical brain implants and VR bodysuits. Their designs were hyper-immersive and fundamentally solitary, which explicitly conflicts with the communal watching they told us they enjoy. They repeatedly voiced concerns about these technologies, differentiating between what they *think* will happen in the future and what they would *like* to happen.

*"I'm scared for the future to come. The telly's not gonna be a thing anymore and everyone's going to be using VR just like tellies … It's better to be sociable. It's better to enjoy things with family. I want TV to stay the same, because it brings people closer together."* 13–17-year-old, female

*"VR movie/viewing experience + microchip for the brain… it attaches to one's face… this device also imitates the taste and smells that are in the video you're watching."* 13–17-year-old, male (figure 3)

*Figure 3. A VR headset with microchip (13–17-year-old, male)*

"…it's an HDMI chip and it has everything you can think of, you just plug it in your head and close your eyes and watch whatever you want." 13–17-year-old, female

"…microchips put into our brains for digital screen (quite bad for health)… glowing sort of eyes (side effect)." 13–17-year-old, male

Child audiences are concerned about what television will become in the future and about their lack of control over their future relationship with it. Younger children want to make TV more familiar by assigning it anthropomorphic attributes, while older children imagine a technologically-determined future of surveillance, dehumanisation and technological control where they have less agency.

## 3: Children want to control their television futures

Children respond to their fears over the future of television by imagining ways they could control it. This manifests through three themes: convenience, portability and customisation. They imagined devices that allow the user to change its appearance or to cover it up and make it 'disappear'. Some future televisions were integrated into familiar objects such as glasses, watches and phones or even given shapeshifting abilities. Several children gave their designs the ability to move, whether it was via wings or wheels, allowing them to be wherever the viewer is (see figure 4).

*Figure 4. Anthropomorphised TV on wheels (9–12-year-old, female)*

to communicate with other people. Others facilitate shared viewing experiences, even if individual viewers are physically distant from each other (figure 5).

*Figure 5. Each circle is a device connected digitally to the others, so people can watch things simultaneously while apart (6–8-year-old, female)*

These preferences for personally tailored television devices did not always conflict with the desire for TV to be something that is shared. Designs often incorporated ways to continue watching television with other people. Some incorporate functions that allow them

Children make television technologies feel less threatening or unfamiliar by imagining futures in which they have more control over their devices and experiences. They imagine a personal relationship with television that gives them choice about what, when and how to watch.

## Conclusion

*Our TV2054: Imagining the Future of Television* report suggests that television remains important to children and they regularly enjoy sharing it with family and friends. However, they have a number of fears about what television could become in the future, particularly in terms of technological developments such as AI, brain-machine interfaces and VR. Younger children respond to these fears by imagining TV sets that are friendly and more human-like. They seek to control this future relationship by reshaping their fears into something that is more approachable though rarely grounded in current technological developments. Older children are resigned to a techno-phobic future but continue to express a desire to retain television's communal quality.

# International Understanding

**Greg Childs OBE**, Director, Children's Media Foundation

In October and November 2024 the CMF was involved in a series of meetings to discover how other countries and in particular public service broadcasting systems are experiencing and handling the shift of viewing by older children and teens away from broadcast services and onto YouTube, TikTok and other video sharing platforms.

The first was at the Young Horizons event in Warsaw. 15 broadcasters including the BBC, NDR (Germany), NRK (Norway), RTÉ (Ireland), TRT (Turkey), VPRO Kids (the Netherlands) and VRT (Belgium) took part.

*Delegates at the Young Horizons event in Warsaw*

All the participants revealed significant loss of audience – as expected – but there were mitigation strategies.

In most cases the aim was to draw the audience back to the broadcasters' players (e.g. the BBC iPlayer) by offering promotional or teaser content on YouTube or TikTok. So a couple of episodes of a popular returning series could stimulate audiences to return to the broadcaster's player for the rest. A couple of the broadcasters revealed they were changing their strategy and abandoning their children's player in favour of a better, age-graded navigation experience for children of all ages on their main player – which the BBC did some time ago.

However, some territories revealed that they placed all of their content on YouTube as well as on their player, to offer the content 'where the children are watching'.

In Latvia and Lithuania, where they don't have the luxury of their own broadcaster players, they have embraced TikTok fully and create public service TikToks. They follow the style and duration of the platform's popular content but provide culturally relevant and age-appropriate material. They admitted adapting to TikTok wasn't easy for experienced programme makers and have instituted a form of apprenticeship scheme whereby young people come into the organisations to learn the principles of public service provision, while sharing their expertise in TikTok and other platforms.

What was clear from the frank and open discussions was that broadcasters – commercial and public service – are losing audience faster than the rate of take-up of their own on-demand services. This remains a concern.

All of the broadcasters admitted that they had changed their positioning on branding. Some focus on key programme brands as the attraction – the IP approach. Others refocus their channel brand as a multi-touch-point cultural service for the young people of their country or region – the social cohesion approach: "this is your place; you speak, we hear you; the things here are all for and about you". With this method, live events feature significantly.

None of the broadcasters was aware of specific initiatives to divert levy funding into content made for kids and young people. And in all cases, there were no government initiatives to regulate the video sharing platforms to improve prominence for public service content.

They also revealed there were no organisations in any of their countries advocating for the children's audience in the political sphere in the way that the CMF does in the UK.

*Discussion at MipJunior in Cannes*

At MipJunior in Cannes, CMF gathered broadcasters, funding organisations, producers and distributors – plus a representative from the only other independent body campaigning for the audience in the children's media field – the Australian Children's Television Foundation (ACTF).

The ACTF outlined recent events in Australia – including continued struggles over funding and a recent arrangement between Screen Australia and YouTube to put some development money into productions intended for the platform. It was thought that the streamers would soon be required to produce children's content in Australia. The plans to prevent people under-16 accessing social media platforms were also discussed (subsequently passed in the Australian parliament), though this was not intended to apply to video sharing sites such as YouTube and TikTok.

The new Canadian 5% levy on streamers was welcomed, but was not without problems in its implementation and has already been challenged in the courts.

US delegates revealed their channels are not immune to the audience migration away from linear broadcasting. And their players, though successful in some cases like Disney+, were struggling to keep up with the 'lost audience'. It was certainly part of the reason for the restructuring and downsizing evident in the large media companies over the last twelve months or so – and this was expected to continue.

Smaller broadcasters like S4C in Wales were passionate about the retention of public service values, but realistic about the need for a shake up in the way content is delivered.

And the BBC revealed that a recent survey of iPlayer use amongst children indicated low usage and awareness.

There was much discussion around how broadcasters and producers could use the new platforms to promote their content – but also more talk than previously of how the platforms could also become the home of their content – in that it was 'home' to their young viewers. A former YouTube insider revealed the ad revenues around officially designated children's content at YouTube were $700m last year, only a small part of the $3.2 billion ad revenue overall. It was not gathered particularly efficiently and the younger audience has always been difficult to advertise to. There was no appetite at YouTube to change the way they share the revenue with children's producers.

What became apparent was that most of the larger media companies find it difficult to discuss the issues in public, as it affects their share value. While – as seemed to be the case in the Warsaw meeting – public service broadcasters in increasingly pressured political circumstances have to be careful about 'special pleading'.

The Animar convention gathered leaders in animation from across the whole of Europe. They were joined by invited broadcasters and funding agencies to discuss a range of policy issues.

CMF outlined the work we have been doing to bring attention to the 'lost audience' to government. All the participants – to a greater or lesser extent – said it was affecting their members' business prospects. Conventional commissioning was drying up and revenue was not being shared.

The EU AVMS Directive is now applied by 15 different European states or regions – in several different ways. Some impose content quotas for streamers, some attach investment requirements to these and some impose levies which basically extract revenue and redistribute it through national or regional funds. The meeting was particularly exercised about two current court cases – both in Belgium – which threaten the powers of AVMS.

In French-speaking Wallonia the government has imposed a levy on the streamers and Netflix has taken the territory to court, claiming that application of a levy through AVMS is contrary to basic European law as it represents a constraint of trade. In the Flemish part of Belgium they have gone further. In the only case of its kind, the Flanders government has levied YouTube, Tik and others. This caused another legal response, as TikTok claims that user-generated content does not fall within the definition of audio-visual content within the AVMS Directive. Both cases tell us something important about how the new platforms will react if their profits are threatened. Results in both cases are months, if not years away. But the readiness to litigate is not a good sign for governments considering taking action – including our own.

The outreach exercise has proved valuable in informing CMF's subsequent conversations with Ofcom and ministers, helping us set the worldwide context of the diminishing reach of the public service – and other broadcasters and the resultant downturn in the children's media industry.

# Reading The Runes

**Jackie Edwards**, Children's Media Specialist, Former Head of YACF, BFI

As usually happens when I write a piece for the CMF Yearbook, I am fresh back from the Voice of the Listener and Viewer (VLV) conference and awards ceremony. Following in the lovely footsteps of *Mixmups* and *The World According to Grandpa*, this year's Best Children's Programme went to the tactile and delicious *Tweedy & Fluff* (also nominated for a BAFTA, a Rockie and already the proud owner of three RTS awards). As *Tweedy & Fluff* creator Corinne Averiss put it, this is a "series made from the heart and not the international board room – reflecting UK heritage and culture, sensitively developed with a deep love and respect for children". As all three shows were in part funded by the Young Audience Content Fund (YACF) it is gratifying that they are recognised for their quality and commitment to public service values.

As well as enjoying the VLV awards, I also learned that I have mystic powers…

## High-end television (HETV) has a problem

I've said before in the *Yearbook* how our problems in children's public service media (PSM) would soon be the problems of all PSM. Call me Cassandra if you like, but VLV featured a panel on funding UK public service broadcasting, with writer and director Peter Kosminsky (*Wolf Hall*), AC Chapter One Managing Director (and *Mr Bates vs The Post Office* Executive Producer) Patrick Spence and television producer Sue Vertue, chaired by Professor Jane Martinson. The panel discussed proposals for addressing financial challenges in the HETV sector – the public service broadcasters (PSB) simply can no longer afford to make high-end UK drama in the inflated cost environment created here by the Streamers.

## HETV has a familiar problem

Given that we have the same (and actually more and worse) problems in children's PSM, we have all thought long and hard about possible solutions.

We know that there are many levers, some harder than others to pull and some faster acting than others, some technically straightforward, but politically tricky.

The HETV folk fell into two funding belief systems: enhanced tax credits versus a 5% streamer levy that would fund a fund to support programmes commissioned by PSBs.

Government should consider all interventions and pull as many of those levers as is possible and as soon as possible. Drama and Children's are the brightest stars in the PSM firmament, but we are in imminent danger of losing both sectors and more broadly, whole swathes of the production industry. With company failure rife and freelance talent leaving the sector in droves there'll be little talent left even for spendy Netflix to make shows in the UK.

The Children's Media Foundation (CMF) put a list of suggestions for intervention to government earlier this year[1]. Rejoining Creative Europe, enhanced tax credits etc are all useful, but if you want to create a targeted, culturally specific (not just 'relevant') solution for delivering PSM, something that could address the needs across genre, target age group and technique, an intervention that delivers value to UK audiences, UK production companies and long term value to the UK economy, there is only one that delivers on societal, cultural, industrial and economic fronts. You don't have to be Nostradamus to predict that I am going to say the word 'fund'.

Bigger Picture's comprehensive evaluation of the Young Audiences Content Fund has just been updated to mark the completion of the fund's wind down process. The fund ran between April 2019 and February 2022, operating two open call strands to support development and production of children's PSM. The total spend across five years (including start up and wind down period) was £44.1M. Projects were expected to meet PSB 'Purposes and Characteristics' identified by Ofcom. In addition, they had to satisfy Fund priorities in eight areas identified by the Contestable Fund White Paper (2018): quality, additionality, diversity, audience reach, plurality, innovation, new voices, and nations and regions.

It was a beautiful (and according to the evaluation, effective, efficient and fair) thing. It enabled VLV winners *The World According to Grandpa*, *Mixmups* and *Tweedy & Fluff* to get into production. The updated evaluation of the YACF revealed that over half of all supported productions had received at least one award nomination across over a hundred award categories.

As well as the quality of the programmes YACF helped deliver, we should also note other things the fund did: 343 hours of nourishing new shows; creating 211,321 job days all across the country (71% outside of London and the southeast), shows that reached and were appreciated by millions of young people, and provided vital support for focussed development, that helped 11% of awarded projects translate into broadcast commissions.

For the £44.1M investment: it delivered hundreds of hours of brilliant new programmes of cultural and societal value; it brought industrial value to hundreds of UK production companies, affording them a period of stability and growth; it allowed structured development of valuable IP; and it offered training and nurturing of talent. The

---

1   Funding Public Service Content for Young Audiences in the UK. CMF-2024-Funding-Public-Service-Content-for-Young-Audiences-in-the-UK-final.pdf

fund also delivered economic value, with a better return on investment than tax credits, including HETVTC. Gross value added (GVA) of £10.10 (£7.25 excluding broadcaster contribution) for YACF. YACF GVA does not include broadcast re-licencing, tourism or licencing and merchandising. GVA for HETV is £6.44, £4.43 for animation tax relief, £3.20 for children's television tax relief and £1.72 for video games tax relief.

By the way, I'm not trying to position this as an either/or argument – all of these are beneficial – I'm just saying if we want a lever that specifically delivers on delivery of PSM and that offers the best economic, industrial and societal value, here it is. It's a fund.

A levy on streamers isn't unreasonable, it's happening in Europe, and if we wanted to utilise a UK comparator… the Eady Levy was imposed on cinema box office receipts which was awash with US content in 1950. The revenue was to support the British film industry and enabled the Children's Film Foundation to produce UK film for UK children. The equation of balancing global with local content wasn't so different then, so no reason not to employ similar mechanics to level the playing field now, eh?

## What next, Mystic Meg?

Our long history of problems in children's PSM are now the problems of HETV, comedy… well, pretty much all of PSM.

This time last year we were blessed with a new government promising change. We'll all have opinions about the nature of some of that change thus far, but for our sector, the mood music at government does seem to have changed, there is interaction, interest, action, conversations being had, opinions being sought. Call me a wide eyed ingenue, but I feel a little *whispers* optimistic about what can happen. People are listening. Maybe they are listening a little more diligently because grown up telly are saying the same things, but whatevs, we are all in the same boat.

But now is the moment we need the people to hear the argument and land it clearly and very loudly. We know, feel and live the problems, let's start shouting solutions, coherently, and together to make sure the listening translates into doing. And soon.

So do as Baroness Floella has instructed for years… email your MP[2], they listen if a lot of people are saying the same thing. Don't be shy.

> "Now is the time, while the government is looking at the problem, let's help them find the solution."

That CMF list of suggestions shared with the government is a useful guide to potential levers to suggest to your MP, but do remember what will really deliver for your business and most importantly the young people of this country. A new fund.

Do it now!

---

[2] https://www.parliament.uk/get-involved/contact-an-mp-or-lord/contact-your-mp/

# Children's Documentary: A Call To Preserve Real Stories

**Dr Tatyana Terzopoulos**, Assistant Professor, RTA School of Media/The Creative School, Toronto Metropolitan University

Documentary media for and about children remains a vital form of storytelling for this special audience. At times, it is a mirror, reflecting aspects of young people's identities, lives, interests (and concerns). Other times, it is a window into the experiences of children from different backgrounds. However, as a form of storytelling for children, children's documentaries continue to be overshadowed by scripted/fictional live action and animated programmes. Despite the abundance of media spanning professionally-produced programs and user-generated content that young audiences can and do engage with, a notable lack of stories that centre real children and honour children's worlds feels especially troubling. With recent funding cuts to broadcasters like PBS in the US as the latest blow to a broader children's media production industry, a form often framed as 'in crisis', children's documentary media production, will likely fade even further into the background. During these particularly volatile times, opportunities for media to thoughtfully include, explore and reflect children's realities is more vital than ever and yet, it has arguably never been at more risk of becoming further deprioritised, I feel compelled to lend my voice – as shaped by my roles as a children's media producer of close to two decades, and as a children's media and media cultures researcher – to advocate for the importance of and explore new directions in children's documentary media storytelling.

Documentary has long been understood as the 'creative treatment of actuality'. This definition, attributed to the Scottish filmmaker and founder of the National Film Board in Canada, John Grierson, in 1936, was attributed to the standalone films produced at the time that were typically focused on specific events or subjects. Given this legacy, it's understandable that the term 'documentary' is often associated with one-off, longer-form storytelling. However, for young audiences, this traditional definition clashes with how children increasingly engage with media – particularly non-fiction – in bite-sized doses, and often created by non-media professionals. This definition also does not fully capture how professionally-produced educational children's media programs often blend factual information and even documentary elements with scripted components into a 'documentary-style' hybrid form, which educate as well as entertain.

In both the UK and Canada, as is the case for many countries around the world, documentary-style content has found a home with public service media outlets (PSMs). Given their cultural mandates and investment in civic representation PSMs have been key to advancing socially meaningful nonfiction content, including for children's populations, that might not otherwise thrive in commercial spaces. Early examples in the UK produced by the BBC such as *Blue Peter* (launched in 1958) and *Newsround* (launched in 1972), blended documentary and magazine formats to reflect children's real lives and interests. *Newsround* in particular was one of the first news programs made specifically for children.

Canada has also had a strong tradition in the non-fiction children's media arena. Through our national and provincial PSMs, generations of children have had access to not only factual/documentary content, but to stories that feature them and involve their participation, especially through the production of interstitial-type content. My own children's media production career was 'launched' when I co-created and produced an award-winning documentary-style series *SWAP-TV*, which blended playful competitive elements from the then-emerging genre of reality TV with more traditional documentary storytelling. The 39-episode series was commissioned by our provincial public service broadcaster, TVOntario and it went on to win a Gemini award in the relatively new non-fiction category in 2004. What felt like a time of great promise for children's non-fiction media, stands in stark contrast to the current state of children's media.

There is a growing demand for documentary media, with Netflix increasing its investment globally in non-fiction stories over the last decade (Lordache et al, 2022), but children's factual content remains underfunded and inconsistently supported across PSMs, globally. Over the years I spent as a freelance children's media professional, it became apparent to me that Canadian children's media producers have frequently found themselves caught between recognising the importance of producing 'diverse' genres of content, including documentary/factual media, and financial realities that lead them to prioritise scripted live action or animated production. Many, including the Shaw Rocket Fund, which is a vital organisation in the Canadian children's media funding and advocacy ecosystem, have been raising concerns about the lack of incentive to support nonfiction programming for over a decade.

Children have long expressed a desire for media that reflects their lived realities and personal experiences. Scholars have emphasised how nonfiction media helps position children as valued societal members, supporting the development of civic identities, empathy and critical thinking. Both my professional production experiences and my research align with these findings. Despite the growing prevalence of social media platforms like YouTube and TikTok – which open up the potential for more perspectives, including children's, to be shared – we are also living in an era marked by misinformation and disinformation. Children now report that they are increasingly struggling to differentiate between fictional drama and factual documentary (Ofcom, 2023).

My experience working with a large number of child participants on productions like *SWAP-TV* provided valuable insights into the impact of nonfiction and documentary-style media on children – both as storytellers and as audiences. The children featured in *SWAP-TV* were given the unique chance to share their lives with the children they swapped places with. The show enabled them to offer their experiences and viewpoints to a wider audience of children across the country. The format of the show was designed to centre children, including providing each participant with the opportunity to craft some relevant 'challenges' for their counterpart during their 'swap'. This was early into the digital media era and for many of these children, participating in the series was a rare opportunity to step into an active storytelling and media participant role at a time when their relationship to media was almost exclusively passive. A child-centred approach became core to my practice as I produced many more documentary-style and educational programs for children in the years that followed – and I have strived to reflect what I consider to be the form's core values: safe participation, real-life relevance and ethical representation. These values now guide my research into co-creation models for non-fiction children's media storytelling – approaches that engage both emerging producers of children's media and children themselves as active participants in the storytelling process.

Despite the volatility in global media industries, children's media professionals continue to create meaningful documentary storytelling for young audiences. Recent standout examples include the European Broadcasting Union (EBU)'s *I Can Do It* series which features children with disabilities completing everyday challenges. Each 15-minute film is produced by a different EBU member and reflects the cultural perspectives of the country while adhering to a shared thematic focus. The series demonstrates the potential of collaborative, international efforts in producing meaningful children's content for diverse audiences.

In Canada, there have been some exceptional child-centered documentary-style programs produced in recent years. Productions such as *It's My Party* and *My Home, My Life* carefully centre children in the storytelling and ensure that diverse populations of Canadian children have the chance to see kids like them, and their traditions, interests, and daily lives centred and celebrated on the screen – and without the need for a streaming service subscription. Another notable program *Old Enough* (based on Japanese reality program-turned-format *Hajimete no Otsukai*) found a way to offer a rare peek into the perspectives, voices and experiences of Canadian preschoolers – while producing a show that would reach wider audience appeal. While it is important to shine a light on children's documentary media success stories, the broader question remains however: how can we continue to support the future of children's documentary media in a landscape increasingly dominated by commercial interests, shifting cultural priorities and dwindling funding.

Agnes Augustin, CEO of the Shaw Rocket Fund argues that structural support is crucial for sustaining a vital industry of children's media producers: the Shaw Rocket Fund suggesting a specific solution – that 20% of Canadian Programming Expenditures be allocated to children's content, with explicit reference to documentary and factual programming. It's clear that a multifaceted approach is necessary – through collaboration, advocacy, and a rethinking of how children's nonfiction storytelling is financed, produced and celebrated. I offer the following considerations towards creating a more inclusive and diverse media ecosystem for children's content:

- **Advocacy for change:** efforts must pivot toward solutions, such as the Shaw Rocket Fund's proposal to earmark funding specifically for children's factual programming.
- **Expand the definition of documentary:** advocate for the expansion of the children's documentary to clearly include emerging formats like short-form, hybrid and participatory content. This expanded definition should be incorporated into funding models and regulatory frameworks to better support diverse storytelling approaches.
- **New co-creation and collaboration models and partners:** encourage new co-production models with stakeholders beyond media who are committed to children's well-being and who recognise the importance of cultivating youth-centered, co-creative storytelling models that place young people at the heart of content creation.

- **Positioning children as collaborators:** it is essential to recognise that children should not only be viewed as passive audiences, but as active collaborators and creators in the media they consume.

Perhaps we must start with recognising children's documentary media as not simply targeting a particular demographic, but as a civic responsibility that plays a critical role in shaping young voices and fostering their engagement with society. Let's commit to *championing* authentic representation, *fostering* co-creative practices, and *elevating* the young storytellers whose voices and experiences urgently need to be seen and heard in our media landscape.

## References

Augustin, A. (2024, September 13). "OPINION: Putting children last". *Kidscreen*. Available from https://kidscreen.com/2024/09/13/opinion-putting-children-last/

Lordarche, C, Raats, T. and Mombaerts, S. (2022). *The Netflix Original documentary, explained: global investment patterns in documentary films and series*. Available from http://dx.doi.org/10.1080/17503280.2022.2109099

Ofcom (2023). *Children and parents: Media use and attitudes report 2023*. Available from https://www.ofcom.org.uk/media-use-and-attitudes/media-habits-children/childrens-media-lives

# Play To Platform: Roblox Is Shaping The Future Of **Kids' Digital Experience**

**David Kleeman**, SVP GLobal Trends, Dubit

Based on its first quarter, 2025 appears to be a 'blox-buster' year for Roblox. The immersive, user-generated content games and experiences platform has repeatedly surpassed its own concurrent-user records (as of this writing, over 13 million players at once). Its daily active user (DAU) average rose 26% year-on-year, to 97.8 million, and players spent a mind-boggling 21.7 billion total hours on the platform – roughly 2.5 million person-*years* – up 30% from 2024.

The numbers are important, but the expanding world of brands on Roblox is even more so. The top entertainment-branded games range widely, from television classics like *Spongebob* and *Ben 10* to global icon brands like Barbie and Hello Kitty. Unless you've been hiding in a cave, you'll have heard of the far-and-away top entertainment brand on Roblox, the bewildering to anyone older than Gen Alpha *Skibidi Toilet*.

While the above are substantially children's brands, Roblox is massive with young adults, as well. Fashion, beauty and sport brands are flocking into the arena, with Maybelline, Fenty, H&M, Givenchy, NASCAR and Manchester City all drawing massive engagement.

As of May 2025, Roblox opened its Commerce API to enable direct sales of physical products from experiences, through Shopify. Given the importance that Gen Z attaches to avatars as vehicles for self-expression, representation and fandom, this promises to reinvent eCommerce. In some ways, it represents a huge step toward a future 'metaverse'.

How did we get here?

## Three generations of user-generated content

Millennials came of age in the first generation of user-generated content (UGC) platforms. Driven by the spread of affordable personal computers, sites like the original Facebook, MySpace and Blogger empowered anyone to become a print and image publisher.

The arrival of camera-equipped phones in the early 2000s presaged the advent of YouTube, democratizing video production and distribution and birthing a competitor to traditional linear motion picture storytelling for late millennials and early Gen Z.

Now, Gen Z (the first truly digital generation) and Gen Alpha (the first born in the mobile digital era) are driving the third generation (and third dimension) of user-generated content. Immersive and explorable worlds like Roblox, Fortnite and Minecraft are fueled by easy-to-use, challenging-to-master powerful software engines, globally and freely available.

> "There's no going back – it's truly a creator economy now"

Three successive generations have now been given tools that disrupt traditional producers and distributors. These tools only get more dynamic and intuitive with the addition of AI. There's no going back – it's truly a creator economy now, and it's growing through a flywheel in which new content draws new audiences, who spend time and money, which attracts even more people to want to build for the platform. Rinse and repeat.

## But Roblox is just a game, right?

Though Roblox has been around since 2007, it's still common to find people who believe it's 'a game'. This even extends to people in the entertainment industry.

The fact is that Roblox is the 'YouTube of Games', with over nine million experiences available and free to play. Its users play an average of 20 games per month.

Many people are further surprised to learn that none of them are created by the company itself. Instead, on Roblox, you'll find everything from simple builds by pre-teens just sticking a toe into Roblox Studio, to deep and challenging titles created by professional studios, drawing millions of players who frequently return.

One benefit of bringing a brand onto a gaming platform is that it is infinitely changeable and expandable. Once a video production is locked, it's finished. With experiences on Roblox and its kin, the creator learns from the platform analytics how users engage and can revise and refresh the world to fans' preferences.

## Down on the corner; up on the server

UGC games are highly social. All players – children through twenty-somethings – meet their friends in favorite games and explore together. Some never even play the experience – they simply hang out in game lobbies and chat with their friends.

The social nature of the UGC platforms also comes through in players' attention to their avatars – their self-representation in the game. In 2024, Roblox players bought 2.2 billion articles of virtual clothing and accessories. Roblox and Fortnite players spent $8 billion combined on avatar items. Together, these two would be the second-biggest fashion company in the world, behind only Gucci at $9.6B, and ahead of Ralph Lauren at $6.3B.

> "For some youth, in-game is their only safe space for 'trying on' various personas or styles"

At a time when Dubit's Trends studies show young people spending more time watching videos and playing games than any other activity but sleep, it's not surprising that one's avatar is an important extension of identity, self-expression and individuality. For some youth, in-game is their only safe space for 'trying on' various personas or styles; for others, it's simply a space for engaging in imaginative role play or signaling a fandom or passion.

In Dubit research with UK youth, girls were found to be more likely to model their avatar after their IRL style or fashion influencers, whereas boys more often chose to mimic sports or social media stars. Over half of those interviewed said they were more likely to buy a virtual item if it copied a real-world favorite brand. With the widespread release of Roblox' eCommerce API, the growth of IRL/in-game 'twinning' and fashion innovation that works in both worlds is certain to grow.

## I'm not a global corporation. Can I still play?

There's room for everyone in the Roblox playground, with options that depend on a set of strategic considerations:

- Are you introducing a new brand or IP, or bringing one that's established to a new platform?
- Do you have an established fan base, and are they already Roblox users?
- Is there a natural 'play pattern' that already is present and popular in existing games?
- Do you want to build something lasting, or for a short-term (e.g, to promote a premiere, or to hold a live event)?
- Do you want to sell or give away merchandise, either in-game or in the real world?

These and other questions can guide you toward one of the multiple means of building presence on Roblox:

- **Standalone game:** the most extensive option, and one that requires a commitment to maintain and update the experience;
- **Virtual event:** concerts, previews/premieres, and other time-sensitive engagements bring in fans and encourage them to invite their friends;
- **Game integration:** if there's an existing, already-successful experience suited to your goals, there's no need to reinvent the wheel, as you can partner for a temporary 'takeover';
- **Immersive retail:** pop-up shops and malls – now able to link directly to Shopify IRL – are growing in popularity, for giving players a chance to explore and try before you buy;
- **Verchandise (virtual merchandise):** a shirt or other branded item bought in one game can usually be worn in all others, enabling your fans to display their passion for your brand or IP throughout the platform.

## Are the ways kids are playing games changing?

One shift becoming increasingly clear is the growing reliance on game subscriptions over individual purchases. With a single AAA console/PC game title now costing as much as £70, many families are opting for services that offer more value. In our recent Trends survey, 53% of kids aged 6–17 had used some form of game subscription in the past month – including PlayStation Plus, Xbox Game Pass, Nintendo Switch Online, and Roblox Premium. Around one in ten used Roblox Premium in the last month alone.

For parents, the model makes sense: subscriptions provide access to a broad library of games for less than half the cost of buying one, even if players don't technically own the games themselves. For kids, subscriptions often come with the added benefit of online multiplayer access, which is increasingly essential for today's highly-social digital play – with 84% of six–17-year-olds saying that they have played games with other people.

In many ways, gaming appears to be following the same arc as television: a move to subscription-based models and content-saturation. Roblox is ahead of the curve, with a platform built around thousands of instantly playable, social experiences, many of which can be played for free with friends.

> "It's about community and connectivity."

In this dynamic environment, Roblox isn't just about play, it's about community and connectivity. Players discover new Roblox games/experiences simply by talking with friends in-game (51%) or by watching streamers (33%). The platform's social architecture turns game discovery into a dynamic, peer-driven process.

## Conclusion: symbiosis on the everything platforms

The UGC platforms – games and video – will continue their rapid growth because of their broad use cases: these are where Generations Z and Alpha (and welcome Beta!) not only watch and play, but also build, explore, compete, collaborate, socialize, communicate and share. Their uses are intertwined, as well: gamers turn to YouTube, TikTok and Twitch for tips and hacks, and to watch favorite player influencers, and video often serves as the discovery engine for finding new immersive experiences. With the growing links to real-life possibilities, these truly are the 'everything platforms'.

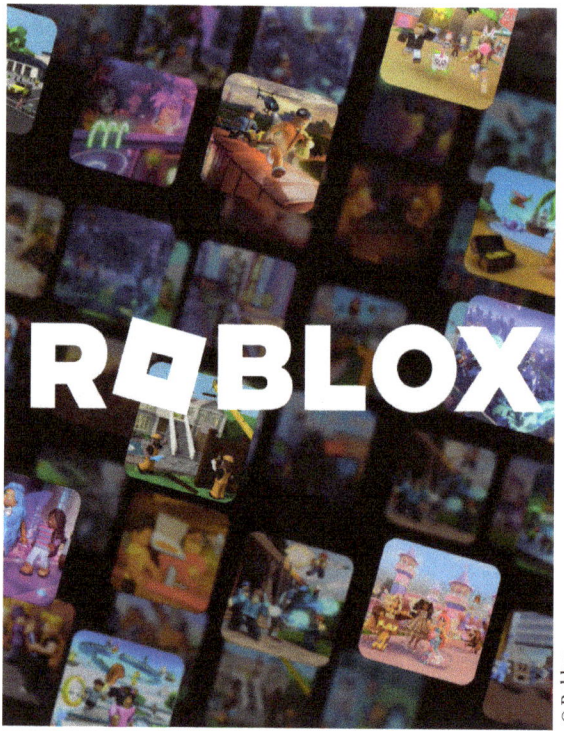

© Roblox

# Trends In Kids' Content

**Karolina Kaminska**, Editor of C21Kids

The children's content industry is constantly evolving as viewing habits change and technology advances. In this article we look at three of the biggest trends currently informing how and what kids are consuming, and how the sector should respond.

## Social storytelling and gaming

Children's programming has gone far beyond the old days of simply sitting in front of the TV, passively watching whatever has been created for the viewer. These days, with the dominance of social media, kids have a wealth of content to choose from that they can not only watch but can really immerse themselves in and interact with. This kind of social storytelling and gaming is taking up more and more of kids' free time, allowing them to participate in the creation of the stories being told.

"This transformation is not merely a trend but a paradigm shift that traditional content creators must take seriously if they wish to remain relevant in the coming years," says executive producer and consultant Rob Doherty, who founded consultancy Relevant Content last year to help bridge the gap between traditional content creation and social gaming.

"The digital age has ushered in a new era where the lines between consumer and creator are increasingly blurred. YouTube may have been the market leading platform for this revolution but social gaming and interactive storytelling on multiple platforms now empower children to become active participants in their own entertainment, not just passive viewers.

"These are not just games; they are expansive, immersive, interactive worlds where children can build, explore and create their own stories. Roblox, in particular, has become a hub for user-generated content, where kids can design their own games, share them with friends and even monetise their creations. Kids today are looking for more than just entertainment; they want to connect, create and share with their peers."

Platforms like Roblox, Minecraft and Fortnite are leading the way in the social gaming space, but are they the future of kids' content and is that where producers should be launching their new IP?

"The implications of this shift, from passive to interactive, are profound. As social gaming and interactive storytelling continue to grow, they are redefining what it means to create content for kids. Future content will likely be less about creating polished, linear narratives and more about providing the tools and environments where kids can create their own stories," Doherty says.

"As creators, we need to collectively educate ourselves on the content children are engaging with and where and how they are consuming it. Those who can successfully navigate this new terrain will not only survive but thrive in the future of kids' content."

## YouTube

Meanwhile, YouTube continues to steal the eyeballs away from traditional platforms, providing a place for children to watch videos on a huge variety of topics and in a multitude of formats, from animation to 'unboxing.' YouTube is heavily criticised by broadcasters and producers for its lack of public-service programming and abundance of low-quality and sometimes harmful content, leading to calls for the platform to start funding projects with public-service values that are socially and culturally relevant.

Earlier this year, YouTube announced an initiative that aims to improve the quality of kids' content found on the platform. The results of the Youth Digital Wellbeing initiative remain to be seen but concerns remain that, at the time of writing, the vast majority of companies involved in the scheme are those with commercial priorities.

Recognising the increasing role YouTube has on kids' lives, most broadcasters and platforms have a presence on the platform and publish certain bits of programming on there to promote their shows. But as YouTube's dominance shows no signs of slowing down, are the traditional players' efforts going far enough or will they have to start commissioning for YouTube?

In Lithuania, public-service broadcaster LRT is already following this approach, by producing and acquiring content specifically for its YouTube channels. "We made a strategic decision to focus on YouTube because over 80% of our audience already spends its time there. Our goal is to be where our viewers are," says Aistė Jūrė, LRT's Head of Children's and Youth Content.

LRT is operating the same model it always has when it comes to producing, funding and acquiring content, according to Jūrė, it's just that the destination for its programming has changed. "We think about these YouTube channels as if they are our own channels," the exec says.

If other broadcasters were to follow in LRT's footsteps, they may cite visibility as a potential issue and how they could ensure their programmes would stand out among the enormous amount of content constantly being uploaded to the platform. While LRT's strategy seems to be going well, Jūrė acknowledges that balancing "viral content with values" while promoting Lithuanian culture is a challenge.

In the UK, BBC Children's and Education is also active on YouTube, although the public-service broadcaster's strategy is to publish excerpts of its flagship shows with the aim of bringing viewers back to its own iPlayer platform to watch them in full.

The broadcaster also recently announced plans to launch live streams and daily bulletins on its Newsround YouTube channel, which are additionally broadcast on CBBC and iPlayer.

"We have, for a long while, been active on YouTube, growing awareness of our content and of BBC iPlayer with its audience. We have to meet our audience where they are, and YouTube is a key service that many of them use," says Director of Children's and Education Patricia Hidalgo.

For its youngest viewers, BBC Children's has a CBeebies YouTube channel which it is building on with themed streams mixing CBeebies House presenters and some of its popular shows.

"By recreating a linear experience that can be accessed at any time we are giving audiences a taster of the great content available in full on BBC iPlayer and we are evolving that strategy to give parents and preschoolers what they want," Hidalgo says.

Aiming to create content that is "YouTube friendly" but also works for iPlayer, BBC Children's launched a series with interactive videos earlier this year that is exclusive to its owned social channels, including YouTube. Featuring host Andy Day as a spin-off to his linear brands, Hidalgo says the show acts as a way for BBC Children's to "test and learn our approach to engage audiences with our content on YouTube and some other third-party services."

"Our mission is to educate, inform and entertain our young audience and to do this we need to meet them where they are, on all platforms including YouTube, with the aim of bringing them back to BBC and specifically to BBC iPlayer where they can view our offer in full."

## Artificial intelligence

The fact anyone can upload videos to YouTube means even more low-quality content is likely on the horizon for the platform with the advent of artificial intelligence (AI).

"There's going to be a lot more cheap and nasty content out there," says John Rice, CEO and Co-Founder of Irish animation studio Jam Media, who adds that he is concerned about "the AI slop that is going to flood the market" and how high-quality, original content can break through it.

"I think it's going to be more and more difficult for actual creators to be found. At what point does content not become human generated but become an AI scraping of everything that's been created up until this point? And what does that do to the evolution of our art?" he asks.

The general consensus among animation companies globally is that AI will be used as a tool to improve efficiencies, rather than to create content or replace human creativity, but fears remain that human jobs will be lost to the AI machine.

"In an ideal world, I would like to see our core employment remain the same, but that we're able to compete, because there are companies that are going to really utilise it and make what we do somewhat as animation studio owners obsolete, potentially in the future," Rice says.

"We will utilise AI in terms of efficiencies but will never let it replace human creativity. What I would like is that we would stay where we are, but our output would increase dramatically."

Also in Ireland, animation studio Turnip + Duck actively uses AI in day-to-day calculations-based tasks but additionally uses it in development to test out ideas before passing them over to the human creative team to do the rest. Co-Founder and MD Colm Tobin has "no doubt" there will be implications for jobs, however.

"We were quite upfront about it and put a policy on our website very quickly when we started to use it," he says. "There are ways we will use it as shortcuts in the creative process, but we have a clear policy that it won't replace the artists we've made all our shows with.

"It's going to definitely change things substantially. Coming from a small company that's always struggling to get our production budgets together, if we can get to screen a little bit quicker and more efficiently and get our stories told in a way that's still ethical, that is an exciting prospect. We will have to see what sort of tools will be developed and what the opportunities are, but I'm excited about the potential for it overall."

It's a tumultuous time for the kids' TV business, and producers and broadcasters are under pressure to stay ahead of the game in order to survive in an increasingly uncertain climate. The phrase 'adapt or die' has been uttered many times over the last couple of years and those wanting to stay at the forefront of children's content would be wise to take heed.

---

# we are family

GOAT

## We're proud to support the Children's Media Foundation and the incredible work they do.

*Children's media plays an important role in preparing our kids for their futures. With a media landscape that's changing fast, their work has never been more necessary.*

helloUK@we-are-family.com

www.we-are-family.com

**Research & Strategy**

**Creative**

**Marketing**

We're a team of curious and creative thinkers specialising in research, strategy, and marketing for children, teens, and families.

### Cymru Greadigol
### Creative Wales

**In Wales, Film, TV and Animation goes to the heart of who we are as a nation – passionate storytellers, with big ideas and a huge amount of creative talent!**

We want to support and celebrate the industry as companies explore new content platforms, projects, and revenue streams.

And with our talented crew, outstanding studio space and funding support we've got it all – including up to 10% grant incentive on top of the UK tax credit offer for qualifying animation projects.

For information about Production Funding support for creative projects, visit our website: **creative.wales/funding-support**

## This is Creative.
## This is Wales.

© Crystal Bears – Enaid Creative

# Animating Minds Project: Triangulating The Age-Appropriate Impact Of Children's Media

**Professor Tim Smith**, Professor in Cognitive Data Science, University of the Arts London, Animating Minds Co-Lead, **Alisa Musatova**, Creative Computing Institute, University of the Arts London, **Dr Claire Essex**, Creative Computing Institute, University of the Arts London, **Dr Rachael Bedford**, Professor in Biological and Experimental Psychology, Queen Mary University London and the Animating Minds consortium.

Modern childhood is mediated by screens. Children learn, play, and socialise through digital media – and fears of negative impacts on development during a critical period of neuroplasticity has led early-years agencies (e.g. UK Chief Medical Officers, American Academy of Pediatrics, WHO) to recommend limits on children's screen time and restrict it to 'high quality' content. Though the recent introduction of the Children's Code (part of UK GDPR law) has nudged the industry to consider age-appropriate design, industry creatives are tasked with figuring out how to ensure their content is appropriate for the developmental stage of their users without clear guidance on how to do so.

This is a provocative problem which cannot be solved by a single discipline. YouTube's recently launched *Youth Digital Wellbeing Initiative* highlights the growing recognition of the need for cross-sector collaboration in creating content that not only entertains but also supports healthy digital development and protects children from harm. However, whilst developmental scientists can advise on the neurocognitive capacities of children, little is known about how these skills apply to media. Similarly, media theorists understand the practice of children's TV creation, but these theories are not empirically validated.

The Animating Minds project is an ambitious two-year long project tackling these growing concerns surrounding children's increasing screen time. By developing an innovative artificial intelligence (AI) tool, we seek to evaluate and predict the effect of digital media content on children's executive functions, a set of cognitive skills essential for self-control and learning that mature across childhood and have been shown to be impacted by screen media – empowering parents, educators, and content creators with valuable insights. Specifically, the project focuses on three –six-year-olds, as this is a key period of neurocognitive development and a transitional age in terms of TV programming.

The project has brought together a diverse team of researchers from the University of the Arts London (UAL), Queen Mary University of London, Birkbeck, Arts University Bournemouth and the University of Brescia. Our combined expertise spans children's animation practice, media theory, developmental psychology, neuroscience and artificial intelligence, ensuring a multifaceted approach to understanding and improving the digital media landscape for young audiences.

Across the project we are looking to understand the ways in which children's media creators tailor their animated content to particular age groups. We will do this by:

- Developing a machine learning (ML) tool to classify children's animation age ratings
- Extending the ML model to predict how animated content impacts three–six-year-olds ability to regulate their behaviour and cognitive processes.
- Designing animations that our model suggests will have a heightened impact on a child's ability to regulate their behaviour and cognition and measuring these impacts using the latest neuroscientific techniques.

The shifting landscape of children's media consumption, particularly the move from traditional broadcast television to platforms like YouTube, adds an important layer of complexity to the Animating Minds project. Today's young viewers are increasingly engaging with short-form, fast-paced, highly captivating content, often created by splicing and rearranging existing episodic content into quickly digestible snippets or compilations. This evolution is not only changing how content is produced and distributed, namely in making the rate of production far quicker, but also how it affects children's attention, comprehension and emotional response.

While Animating Minds is designed to assess the effect of traditional, broadcast-quality children's television, we also aim to explore how these tools can be adapted to new forms of digital animation, including the rapidly changing platform-native content designed for particular age groups. By doing so, we hope to contribute to a deeper understanding of how the animation industry is evolving, and how children's developmental needs can continue to be supported in this ever-changing media environment.

> "Existing age classification systems offer helpful starting points … [but] they may not fully reflect the nuanced developmental differences."

Existing age classification systems – such as the systems used by the BBFC and IMDb, or the age guidance provided by Common Sense Media – offer helpful starting points for understanding what might be appropriate for children. However, these systems often group a wide range of content under broad categories and primarily rely on content-level assessments, such as themes, language, or violence, rather than considering low-level features like visual complexity, pacing, repetition, etc. As a result, they may not fully reflect the nuanced developmental differences in executive function between, for example, a three-year-old and a six-year-old.

Perhaps obviously, the experts who have the greatest ability to gauge media's 'age-appropriateness' are the creatives behind the production of the animated content. The UK children's media industry has been at the pioneering edge of international children's TV and animation for decades. Child- and adult-directed content differs radically in style (e.g. animation vs. live-action, slow versus fast pace) and embedded learning (e.g. phonics, numeracy, diversity), but the impact of these approaches is not empirically validated. A route to understanding 'age appropriateness' therefore lies in working with creatives to formalise, test and solidify their intuitions to inform the creation of objective computational tools.

Creatives' insights into all aspects of children's animated media (from colour palette to storytelling decisions, visual styles to emotional tones, background sound to thematic elements) will be gathered through a series of knowledge exchange sessions, first in the form of one-to-one interviews, followed by a set of group discussions. These sessions will go beyond surface-level observations, delving into the tacit knowledge and instinctive choices that experienced creatives draw upon in their work. These insights will inform the design of our computational tool, ensuring it is deeply grounded in real-world creative practice.

We are currently looking to connect with a diverse range of professionals working across the children's animation industry. This includes not only writers, directors and animators, but also editors, producers, storyboard artists, character designers and others involved in shaping content for young audiences. If you work in this space and are interested in contributing your insights to the Animating Minds project, we'd love to hear from you!

We are also in the process of collating a collection of children's animation content currently available via broadcast, video on demand and streaming platforms, to support the machine learning objectives of the project. Our aim is to ensure that the content accurately reflects the range of content children are actually watching today. (All the data and machine learning models will be made open source at the end of the project.) If you are able to contribute material or make recommendations for inclusion, your support would be greatly appreciated and highly valuable to the research!

Please feel free to get in touch with us directly to express your interest or to learn more about how you can get involved!

### *Contact details*

*Email: cci.animatingminds@arts.ac.uk*

*Website: https://www.arts.ac.uk/creative-computing-institute/research/projects/animating-minds*

*Thank you to other contributors from the Animating Minds project: Mick Grierson, Alex Oakley, Aldrich Pan, Paola Pinti, Mattia Savardi, Paul Taberham, Freya Woolford, Rachael Bedford*

# Pablo: Next Level. What We Do Matters

**Gráinne McGuinness**, Creative Director, Paper Owl Films

*Pablo has joined a new, mainstream school. It's complicated.*
*He's working it out one drama at a time.*

Preschool *Pablo* brought joy to children all over the world. *Pablo*'s transformation into an iconic international show for older kids, brings the audience into a fresh, unique perspective that seeing things differently brings to the everyday. It's weird, it's wild and it's full of funny. *Pablo: Next Level* is bursting with all the wacky humour of the modern eight-year-old's experience. The stories not only shine a light on the autistic perspective, they blow the lid on how we see ourselves in the world.

**CHANGING THE WORLD.** My Dad used to say that it was pointless to do the same thing today that you did yesterday and expect a different result. If we keep looking at things in the same traditional way, communicated by the loudest voices, we will keep doing the same things and nothing will ever change. We need the engagement of all kinds of minds in the world if we are going to create better results for ourselves. When we see things in different ways, we can see new ways forward.

**STORIES MATTER.** Screen content harnesses everything in our storytelling toolkit. It has real power. We are the grown ups in charge of that on-screen storytelling for children, the power to help change their world in our hands. What we do matters. We have the tools to create a positive impact – to raise the happiness levels of children and help them become the powerful champions of a better world.

**PABLO.** Following the stand out success of *Pablo* for preschoolers, spin-off series: *Pablo: Next Level* is a 40 x 11-minute series which we are co-producing with Cake in association with Crayola for BBC Children's and RTÉjr. This is a comedy series for five–eight-year-olds that sees Pablo navigating the chaos of school, one drama at a time.

Pablo's perspective allows us to look at school in a whole new way – and when we do this we see how silly the small stuff we sweat is, how nonsensical the rules are – and how often they CHANGE! Pablo gives us fresh eyes to look at the details of how the school world works for children and to see just how the smallest of changes can make a huge difference when it comes to all kinds of minds engaging together, collaborating, creating and solving problems!

It's a quirky angle for comedy. Laughing helps us see things differently, feel good about what we need to do to make room, make change. Having fun, creating joy is the heart of empathy and conflict resolution. The heart of making the world a better place.

On-screen representation in children's television matters deeply. It shapes how children see themselves, each other and the world. Much loved neurodivergent characters reflect the audience – one in 100 children in the world are diagnosed autistic – it's so important for them to see themselves on screen – and it's vital for all children to engage because that creates understanding, and from understanding grows empathy and growth.

For neurodivergent audiences, Pablo's adventures and antics in the school world offer a powerful mirror. These stories affirm that their thoughts and challenges are real and shared. Pablo is a role model really – we celebrate his joys, his creativity and how he uses that creativity to strategise the world.

Pablo's friends are a mixed bunch. Through one misunderstanding or misadventure at a time, they grow in love and understanding. It's all so warm and funny and a beautiful way to model inclusive classrooms and playgrounds, social interaction, patience(!) and flexibility through different ways of thinking.

The Book Animals of his inner world personify different aspects of his personality and put the traits of autism on screen for the audience. For example, Noa has a lot of social anxiety, Mouse is sensitive to sounds and smells, Tang's energy makes it hard to contain his impulses, Wren loves flapping, Llama is echolalic and Draff is a very black and white thinker.

**COMEDY MATTERS.** *Pablo: Next Level* is written by autistic comedians and storytellers. They are bringing untold stories to screen in really funny ways – the whole style of the show is quirky with mixed media and animation reflecting Pablo's processing style and how his art and imagination helps him work through the challenges and share the joys.

*Pablo: Next Level* will cut through for its comedy and the treasure inside that comedy wrapper is a shift in the media landscape – not only putting autistic creativity on screen to be loved and sharing how engaging, joyous and fun it is to have a world that includes all kinds of minds collaborating together.

**REPRESENTATION MATTERS.** *Pablo*'s success is a testament to the power of storytelling that is rooted in lived experience and meaningful collaboration with neurodivergent creators. Representation of neurodiverse characters like Pablo is not just a positive step – it's essential.

Seeing yourself represented validates your existence and builds self-worth. Children who never see people like themselves in positive, central roles can feel invisible. We need these children – they have a massive contribution to make to a better world. Helping them feel seen is really important to their self esteem.

Diversity is natural. We are all diverse. It's not an exceptional, separate thing although traditional representation on-screen rooted in the dominant view may have led us to feel that way. Diverse representation helps children understand and accept all kinds of people – fostering empathy, reducing prejudice and supporting more inclusive thinking as they grow. The content we make has such power when you think about that.

Pablo is a role model for success: he's not perfect in an ideal world, and neither is anyone around him. They are muddling through, having fun, laughing and growing, remembering the joys and working through the challenges. Pablo and his friends are trying and failing, achieving goals and dealing with it when they don't. He's a hero – championing the effort, expanding his sense of what's possible and thus expanding the audience's sense of what's possible.

The content we create is one of the most powerful tools in shaping what is considered 'normal' acceptable, or desirable. In shifting cultural norms it can contribute to real social progress – because if we see it we can change it. When Pablo succeeds we believe that success is possible for ourselves and others. When a small change to the norm helps him succeed we celebrate the power of simple things. Inclusive affirming representation benefits both the autistic viewer and society as a whole.

**SHAKING IT UP MATTERS.** We need to shake things up. Always! Challenge what we are doing, how we are doing it – ask ourselves if we really are getting it as right as we think we are and how we could do it better. Pablo is a creative little boy who opens up a world of creative processing to audiences and that encourages engagement, collaboration and joy for younger viewers in a world that strives to meet everyone's needs – not just those of the majority or the loudest voices.

**CREATIVITY MATTERS.** Representation on screen helps audiences see the world in different ways. This kind of thinking breeds innovation. People with different ways of perceiving and processing the world come up with new things, fresh ideas. For *Pablo*, that has meant a storytelling revolution – with fresh, funny, original storytelling on screen that we haven't seen before. It's the holy grail of content creation to find original voices, new stories – and *Pablo* keeps on doing this because there is a treasure trove of neurodiverse stories that have not been told through traditional content channels. It's a creative joy to see these come to screen and to continue to find exciting and important ways to express fresh perspectives in the world.

A world that includes a variety of perspectives is one that is better able to adapt to change and uncertainty. In practice we've been so fortunate at Paper Owl to see first hand how exciting team performance is with varied thinking styles in there. Bringing different ways of thinking and seeing together really does help you create truly new content yes, but also new ways of doing things in the studio. So producing *Pablo* continues to bring mindset change and innovative problem solving in how we go about producing the content too.

Inclusive content enriches communities, drives innovation, builds a more just, creative and compassionate world. This is more than passive on screen representation – this is building real practical advantages for the audience and the world they will grow up to create.

# Maddie + Triggs: It's Amazing What You Hear When You Take The Time To Listen

**Colm Tobin**, Managing Director, Turnip + Duck

I should start by saying this: I'm probably not the guy you'd pick to make a groundbreaking, values-driven, inclusive preschool series. At least, I wouldn't be the obvious choice.

Back in the late 90s and early 00s, I was cutting my creative teeth making deeply silly, often offensive satirical cartoons with my childhood collaborator Aidan O'Donovan and some other college friends. Inspired by *The Day Today*, *Brass Eye*, and with a visual palette owing a lot to Terry Gilliam's early Python work, we prided ourselves on equal-opportunity offending. No sacred cows. No holding back. No regrets… well, actually loads of regrets, but that's another story.

We made web cartoons featuring Irish politicians in jacuzzis with Joseph Stalin and Margaret Thatcher. We featured the dead heroes of the 1916 Rising careering around Dublin in an *A-Team* van. Our aesthetic was part *South Park*, part student house share, with a generous side serving of Buckfast. It was crass, chaotic and, by some miracle, it caught on and launched our careers in animation – quite a feat for two guys who had only ever successfully drawn one thing: the dole.

So how did I end up here, co-creating a joyful animated musical preschool series for CBeebies and RTÉjr? Honestly, I'm still not entirely sure. But if I had to put a pin in it, I'd say that sometimes a project chooses you. And when it does, your only job is to try not to mess it up.

*Maddie + Triggs* didn't start with a pitch deck or a style bible, as was the case on many of our previous shows. It started with sound. In 2020, while the world was busy baking banana bread, we built a 15-episode podcast in our attics. It was a small, DIY labour of love featuring a seven-year-old girl named Maddie who happened to

© Turnip + Duck

be vision-impaired, her adorable labradoodle Triggs, and their magical, musical adventures in the town of Higgledy-Piggledy.

It was playful, funny, and entirely audio-led – a throwback to the kind of storytelling Aidan and I had grown up making, long before anyone handed us a budget or a deadline. It gave us the chance to take up our musical instruments again and make some tunes with a small team of like-minded collaborators. We did most of the voices ourselves. It was multitasking gone mad.

What made this project different was our mission:

> **If two children, one sighted and one vision-impaired, sit down to watch the show, neither should have a lesser experience.**

That idea came from a chance comment by our friend Óran O'Neill at RTÉ, who had lost his sight as an adult and helped us create the audio description on our previous series *Critters TV*. He mentioned that *Critters* worked surprisingly well in audio because the humour was so dialogue-led. But we had never really considered a vision-impaired audience. In fact, the audio description for that show was done as an afterthought, a contractual obligation with our funders.

That got us thinking – what if we started there? What if sound wasn't an afterthought, as it is so often in animation? What if it became the central focus of our development? And what if we considered a vision-impaired audience from the very beginning?

We realised pretty quickly that making a show with a vision-impaired lead character meant we had a responsibility. Both Aidan and I aren't vision-impaired. This is not our story to tell. And we didn't want to charge into this territory with the clumsy confidence of two middle-aged white knights on a diversity side quest. So we didn't.

Instead, we took a leaf from Maddie's book and started to, well, listen.

We partnered with Vision Ireland and met with blind and vision-impaired children and their families. One moment that stayed with us was hearing how rarely these kids saw (heard!) themselves reflected on-screen – and when they did, it was often only in the context of their disability, or in a sad, issue-led storyline. What they wanted was joy. Fun. Characters who just happened to be like them, but who were busy having adventures, telling jokes, singing songs.

We worked with our partners Angel Eyes in Belfast, experiencing their EmpathEyes VR simulator to better understand different types of sight loss. They were hugely supportive as we developed the show's unique aesthetic, rooted in Universal Design principles. Our animation partners at Sun & Moon in Bristol brought that vision to life with incredible care and craft. We learned that by making something more accessible for one audience, you end up making something better and more beautiful for everyone.

Our first hire on the series was a digital access and accessibility consultant, Shelley Boden, who helped us build inclusion into our production from day one, on-screen and off. With Shelley's help, we brought blind and vision-impaired talent into the team, and we launched the Listen

Hear programme, training up ten new vision-impaired writers over the course of the production. Four of them will earn their first full writing credits on *Maddie + Triggs*, including our audio description lead Óran O'Neill, which is a lovely full circle. All the lyrics on the show are written by Dena Diamond, a blind comedy writer from the US, who works closely with our writers and musical director so the music and stories are fully intertwined.

*Maddie and Triggs mix up a 'bonkers cake'!*

From the start, it felt like there was a gentle breeze behind this project, pushing us toward brilliant collaborators and generous supporters. But it hasn't all been smooth sailing. This kind of work takes time. It takes funding. It takes real coordination across organisations that don't always move at the same pace. And when you're also trying to keep a small business afloat in a challenging industry, it can be extremely tough. But the work is worth it. And we feel like we are only scratching the surface. We're committed to deepening and expanding this ethos in future series of *Maddie + Triggs*, and beyond.

Now, this isn't to say we've abandoned all nonsense at Turnip + Duck. We absolutely reserve the right to make rude, scatological silliness just for the joy of it. But *Maddie + Triggs* has changed us. It's shown us that accessibility and inclusion aren't niche concerns. They're not boxes to tick. They're creative engines.

They make for better storytelling. Happier teams. Stronger work. And, maybe unexpectedly, they make you a better person along the way.

We've seen the impact of this show – not just on kids, but on the grown-ups making it. Writers, animators, producers, musicians – all coming away with a deeper understanding of difference, and a greater appreciation of how sound, story and representation can sing in harmony.

In a world where some forces are weaponising language against DEI or EDI policies, it's never been more important to double down on shared values in kids' content. Seriously, if we can do it, anybody can. As Maddie says:

> **"It's amazing what you hear when you take the time to listen."**

It really is.

# Ultra Access: Unlocking The Magic Of TV

**Rebecca Atkinson**, Writer and creator, Ultra Access

Could Ultra Access™ unlock language and stories for preschool children who have been left behind by children's industries?

Earlier this year, 5's Milkshake! show *Mixmups* launched Ultra Access™, an interactive TV service offering viewers the ability to personalise their viewing experience with options including turning down the background sound and simplifying the visuals; taking TV access beyond the traditional subtitles, audio description and sign language and into the hands of the viewer.

Acquiring language is like building a house – there are foundation blocks which must be laid before you can build anything higher. You need a ground floor before you can proceed to build a first floor, second floor or even a third. Each level of language comprehension rests on the shoulders of the one beneath.

As babies, we start with no language, our caregivers lay the foundations and begin to label items: "That's a ball, that's a cat, that's an apple". We learn that everything has a name. Once the foundations are laid, we can go on to learn about categories: "A cat is an animal. An apple is a fruit."

Many parents will remember the 'point and label' stage of their child's language development. Their delight at pointing their little toddler finger and expressing their knowledge by labelling an object or person, "Mamma, Mamma, ball, ball." Soon after, they begin to talk in sentences to express their knowledge, wants and needs: "Daddy do it!" "My [sic] want it!"

But what happens when a child is born deaf? What if you can't hear the words that are being used to label the objects around you and your caregivers are not versed in the communication methods you need in order to learn?

There are 45,000 deaf and hard of hearing children in the UK and 90% of them are born to hearing families who rarely can already sign themselves (and many cannot afford to learn as there is no government funding to support parents of deaf children), leaving deaf children at risk of language deprivation from the get-go. If they struggle to get the foundations of language, they can't build the next layers of comprehension easily, they will struggle to communicate their needs, understand the world around them, keep up with peers, read, follow stories and develop positive self-esteem. Early years language deprivation has lifelong consequences.

Whilst writing the stories for *Mixmups*, I wondered how deaf children would access my work. I had grown up partially deaf myself, before subtitles were widely available and had first-hand experience of my little brain trying to make sense of stories on TV from the fragments of words I had managed to catch.

Today we have widespread use of captions, but most preschoolers are unable to read, so subtitles are ineffective for this audience. Whilst all 52 episodes of *Mixmups* are available with British Sign Language, most preschool deaf children won't yet have developed sign language at the level needed to fully understand everything being conveyed either. How do these children fully access and understand preschool content? The short answer is, they don't. These children are being underserved by the very industries which exists to entertain and educate them: kids industries.

I wondered if there was anything I could do to innovate in this space and bring deaf children into the world of *Mixmups* on their own terms. I began to research the literacy attainment of other groups of disabled children and found similar concerns.

There are around 30,000 blind and visually impaired children in the UK. Whilst all 52 episodes of *Mixmups* are available with audio description overlaid, there isn't the aural space between dialogue to tell the child what the characters look like, what the world looks like or give them any context or detail, it merely describes the action. Visual impairment can lead to language delay in a different way to deafness due to lack of visual cues and experiences. If a blind child has never seen or touched a real duck, only a toy one, they may

*Small subtitles, BSL interpreter*

*Emotional support from moodily clouds, with BSL and subtitles added*

*Larger subtitles and simplified visuals*

assume that all ducks are hard, shiny and made of plastic. They have no visual cue that there are multiple types of duck in the world unless they have interacted directly with them. For a blind child to have full access, they need to experience things on a multi-sensory level, to understand that a real duck is soft and feathery and a toy duck is something quite different, but confusingly, they are both called ducks!

In addition to deaf and visually impaired children, there are as many as 300k children in the UK with a learning disability and an estimated 14% of children are thought be neurodivergent. Both these groups have distinct access needs which are not met by traditional TV access offerings of subtitles, audio description and sign language.

Access doesn't always mean sensory access in the moment of viewing. For many disabled children it means preparation before you watch the show to embed a level of understanding before the show has even begun. Something I understand personally. I always google a film's synopsis before watching and read the script before enjoying a theatre performance. Knowing what is going to happen helps my brain to piece together the action and get the meaning of the story, even if I don't catch every line of dialogue.

Parents and teachers of children with autism and additional learning needs often use social stories to prepare a child for an unfamiliar event like a trip to the doctors. They break the upcoming event down into small steps and use simple pictures to support understanding and prepare the child for what to expect. After surveying parents and finding that they wanted this to be done for TV shows too, I contacted Stornaway, a Bristol-based tech company who specialise in interactive TV and together with Mackinnon and Saunders (producers of *Mixmups*) we began devising Ultra Access™ powered by Stornaway.

5's Milkshake! commissioner, Louise Bucknole, took a leap of faith when she commissioned Ultra Access™ as part of the original *Mixmups* commission. It was an unknown entity, just an idea at the time, but in doing so Milkshake! has unlocked the power of language and TV stories to an underserved segment of their audience in a global first.

Viewers can now choose from a raft of access options and mix up their bespoke viewing experience of *Mixmups*. With options including a full audio described introduction to the characters, premise and sets, a list of sensory props to hold whilst watching, emotional regulation support, episode storylines, the choice between Makaton sign language and British Sign Language, including key signs to watch and learn before an episode, the number of ways to to watch with Ultra Access™ are mind boggling. There are over 4,000 permutations depending on what you add into your personalised mix.

Whilst *Mixmups* is the test case, Ultra Access™ powered by Stornaway can be easily applied to other shows. What if brands like *Bluey*, *Peppa Pig* and *Paw Patrol* all offered ten episodes with Ultra Access™? What if CBeebies and other global public service broadcasters committed to a small percentage of their output with Ultra Access™? Disabled preschoolers would start to have real choice and the means to at last connect with the magical stories of our industry. I urge commissioners globally to consider supplementing their current access offers with Ultra Access™. They have the power to unlock stories and language for 150 million disabled kids worldwide and place power back in their hands by enabling them to be entertained and educated on their own terms. The tech is there; now it's up to commissioners to apply it and begin serving all preschool children.

# More Than Metrics: Youth Marketing For **Passions And Fandoms**

**Maxine Fox**, Managing Director, Giraffe Insights and **Sam Clough**, Global Head of Strategic Research and Insights, SuperAwesome

*This is a digest of research carried out by SuperAwesome and Giraffe Insights. The full report,* Fandoms & Passions – The Antidotes to Hyper-Fragmented Youth Audiences, *is available online.*

The youth audience has never been more powerful or more difficult to reach. In 2025, the challenge for brands lies not just in capturing attention but in building authentic, lasting connections with Gen Alpha and Gen Z. As culture fragments and platforms multiply, young people continue to evolve faster than ever before. It's no longer enough to know where they spend their time; brands must understand what truly drives them.

SuperAwesome conducted research with Giraffe Insights to uncover how brands can better connect with kids and teens, not just through content and campaigns but through emotional resonance. The key insight? Passions and fandoms are the golden threads that connect young audiences to the brands they love.

## Why this matters now

Youth culture is moving at speed, shaped by ever-changing digital environments and a growing desire for personal expression. Traditional data sources fall short when it comes to under-18s, leaving marketers with blind spots. And with younger audiences more selective and values-driven than ever, even the most well-intentioned campaigns can fall flat.

To engage these audiences meaningfully, brands need to shift their lens from broad demographics to specific passions and fandoms

that reflect identity, values and emotional needs. These are the factors that make or break brand loyalty in a crowded, competitive space.

## What our research revealed

Our multi-market study of nearly 4,000 young people explored the powerful connection between passions, fandoms and brand affinity. The findings were clear:

- 74% feel more connected to brands that share their passions.
- 73% feel more positive about brands that collaborate with something or someone they're a fan of.
- 67% believe brands could do more to help them feel connected.

Young people are hungry for connection, but it has to feel real. Brands that align with their passions and tap into the fandoms they care about are more likely to earn that connection and build lasting relationships.

## Age and stage still matter

It's important to note that a child's development means that their age and stage still remain incredibly important. When it comes to connecting with kids, we can't abandon demographics completely especially when it comes to age. However, the notion that delivering a campaign aimed at four–nine-year-olds is enough to reach a relevant audience is outdated, and the most successful brands will understand the need to go much further than this to drive efficiencies.

This is in part because kids are evolving much faster than their older counterparts and things they like naturally change over time. Knowing when to tap into different passions and fandoms is key to leveraging them correctly.

Data from our research also shows that while both passions and fandoms endure and, in many cases, deepen as kids age, fandoms are acquired

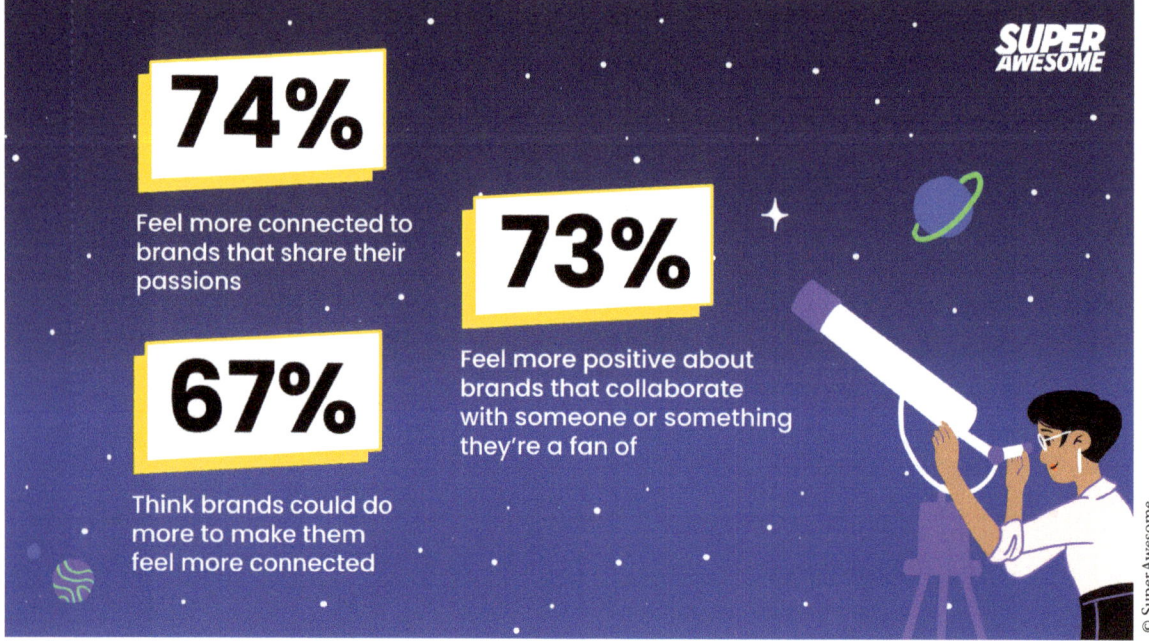

and shed more frequently than passions, which tend to inform the fandoms themselves.

On average, young people have four passions at any one time while they have two fandoms and this makes sense when we consider the financial, social and time investment required for some fandoms (think being a Swiftie or a fan of Manchester United, for example, versus enjoying music or football).

## Rethinking how we define audiences

Whilst age and stage are important, demographics alone only scratch the surface. If you're marketing to four–nine-year-olds, you're missing the deeper emotional and cultural nuance that defines this generation.

Instead, we need to look at the whole picture:

- What motivates young people?
- What gives them joy, pride or a sense of belonging?
- How do they use their interests to form identity and connect with others?

Passions and fandoms answer these questions. They're not just pastimes. They're frameworks for how young people experience the world.

© SuperAwesome

## Passions vs. fandoms?

Passions are deep personal interests that help young people grow. These could be gaming, sports, arts, coding, etc. They offer joy, help build skills and contribute to a sense of self.

Fandoms, on the other hand, are more social. They're built around shared love for a particular piece of content, celebrity or brand. Think Taylor Swift, Minecraft or Star Wars. Fandoms create community, offering young people a way to connect with others who feel the same.

Kids engage with both daily: three in five say they connect with their passions every day and over half say the same about their fandoms. But while passions are more enduring, fandoms shift more frequently.

## From identity to belonging

When brands align with passions, they tap into something personal. When they engage with fandoms, they gain access to a shared experience. Together, these entry points allow brands to connect with youth in a way that's meaningful and memorable.

Let's take LEGO as an example. A child passionate about creativity and building might already be a LEGO fan. When LEGO partners with Fortnite or Star Wars, it adds a new layer of connection, merging personal passions with collective fandoms and inviting kids to explore new worlds with others like them.

## A smarter framework for brands

What does this mean for brands and how they look to connect with young people? Here are four principles brands should consider adopting to engage young audiences more effectively:

**1. Go beyond demographics**
Age and gender are not enough. Brands need to understand values, behaviours and emotional needs of their audience. What drives them to engage? What matters most to them? Deeper insight creates more effective campaigns.

**2. Be authentic, not opportunistic**
Young audiences are savvy. They can spot inauthentic marketing from a mile away. A logo stuck onto the latest trend won't cut it. Brands need to integrate thoughtfully into the content, creators and communities that kids care about. Show up in ways that reflect their values.

**3. Use fandoms to drive community**
You don't need to create a fandom from scratch. Instead, join the ones your audience already loves. Collaborate with creators, launch exclusive drops, or show up in the digital spaces they already inhabit, from Roblox and Fortnite to YouTube and TikTok. Fandoms are where young people connect, and where brands can become part of the conversation.

**4. Invest in long-term loyalty**
Brand loyalty starts early. By the time kids hit their teens, their preferences are often well established. If you're not connecting with them now, you risk being left behind. This isn't about short-term wins, it's about long-term brand equity.

Ask yourself: Do you still use the same toothpaste or wear the same sneaker brand you did as a teen? Chances are, those early relationships stuck. Today's kids will form similar connections with the brands they encounter now.

## The path forward

We believe that the future of youth marketing lies in empathy, understanding, and authenticity. Through years of research into youth culture, we've seen firsthand how meaningful connections are made, not just with eyeballs, but with hearts and minds.

> "Meaningful connections are made ... with hearts and minds."

To build lasting connections with Gen Alpha and Gen Z, brands must dive beneath the surface. Understand their values. Learn what excites them. Join them in the spaces they care about and most importantly, show up with sincerity.

Passions and fandoms aren't fleeting trends, they're emotional anchors. And in a world of constant change, they're one of the few reliable ways to create real, lasting relationships with the next generation of consumers.

# Battle For The Boys: **Evolving Masculinity** On-Screen

**Dr Yalda T Uhlis**, Founder & CEO, UCLA Center for Scholars & Storytellers

Adolescence is a critical time for identity formation, and in a digital world where young people (in the US) report spending an average of six–nine hours a day consuming entertainment media (film, television, video games etc.) (Council on Communications and Media, 2016; Common Sense Media, 2019), what they see on screens – big and small – influences how they will act, what they will believe and who they will become.

For too long, we've sold them outdated and incomplete versions of what it means to 'be a man'. In one large-scale content analysis of teen-oriented films across three decades, researchers found that male characters committed a staggering 86% of all aggressive acts on-screen (Coyne et al. 2010). Another study of television content revealed that boys and men are often overrepresented in depictions of risky behaviors, such as substance abuse, reckless driving and physical violence. These portrayals have real consequences and the statistics show us just how dire they truly are.

Men are three times more likely than women to die from suicide, alcohol poisoning or drug overdoses. They account for over 98% of all mass shootings in the United States. And they are lonelier than ever. According to the BBC Loneliness Experiment, a global study of over 55,000 people, men reported higher levels of social isolation than women – especially younger men under the age of 25.

It's not just the data that's concerning; it's what boys themselves are saying. In a Plan International USA survey of over 1,000 boys ages ten–19 in the US, 44% said they believe society expects them to be aggressive or violent when angry. Just 2% said society values honesty and morality in boys. And a shocking 63% of men said they believe they are encouraged to 'seize sex whenever they can'.

It's time for a rewrite: boys and men deserve better examples of who they are and who they can become on-screen, so they can truly live up to their full potential off-screen. Entertainment industry professionals have the power to help.

## Move beyond stereotypes

According to research from Equimundo, the most prominent stereotype about masculinity depicted in children's television is of boys and men as aggressors – and on the whole, male characters are shown as less likely to express emotions in healthy ways than female characters.

Storytellers can help flip the script by showing male characters who express a wide emotional range – not just anger – and who are able to resolve conflict in non-violent ways. They should also consider showing men thriving in a variety of roles and activities, not just those considered traditionally masculine. This can mean showing men as caretakers or nurses; participating in household chores like laundry, cooking and cleaning; and boys painting or playing with dolls.

## Show healthy friendships

Boys need deep, meaningful friendships just as much as anyone else. In fact, research led by the Center for Scholars & Storytellers shows that boys with close friendships are less prone to depression and more likely to live longer lives. Content creators can help provide a model for healthy male friendship by showing male characters who are vulnerable, thoughtful and caring for those around them – depicting male friendships rooted in empathy, trust and emotional openness. This can include showing boys confiding in each other, comforting one another during hard times and standing up to a friend when they cross a line with bullying or violence, rather than portraying men and boys merely as bystanders.

On-screen male friendships don't only have to be limited to being only with other men. Normalising platonic relationships between boys and girls has been long overdue. Not every story needs to pivot toward romance. And in fact, most young people don't want it to.

In several studies at the Center for Scholars & Storytellers, we've seen young people report over and over again that they are more interested in seeing stories about diverse friendships than romance, and the vast majority don't believe sex and romance are necessary to advance the plot. Showing cross-gender friendship where boys and girls play together and confide in each other without undertones of romantic or sexual tension can help teach young men from an early age how to build relationships based on respect.

## Embrace nuance

Just like any other demographic, men and boys are not a monolith. And when it comes to rewriting narratives around masculinity, showing characters with depth and nuance remains key.

After all, masculine traits don't have to exist on a binary. We can show men as both strong and vulnerable – both courageous and confident enough to ask the girl out, as well as gracious and mature enough to handle rejection – both adventurous and ambitious enough to follow

© Photo by Alexandr Podvalny on Unsplash

their passions, as well as grounded enough to fulfill their responsibilities and stand in their convictions. Men are capable of so much more complexity than we've afforded them through tropes of stoicism and ego. It's time for us to start showing them that on-screen.

Across the board, our research at the Center for Scholars & Storytellers shows youth are craving characters who exist beyond extremes – who are able to show a full spectrum of gender identity and expression and are able to experience a wide variety of complex emotions and relationships. And it turns out when the industry delivers on that, it's not only better for young people and better for society, it also ends up being better for the project's bottom line. Evolving narratives around masculinity advances the greater good while also making content more creative, more interesting and more appealing to young people.

With every script we write, every character arc we map, every line of dialogue we approve, we are sending messages to millions of young viewers about what is acceptable, admirable and aspirational. We have the power to ensure those messages reflect the best of who we are and the best of who we hope boys will become. It's up to us to use that power wisely to create both better stories and a better shared future for all.

*For more research-backed insights on how to evolve depictions of boys and men on-screen visit scholarsandstorytellers.com/boys.*

## References

NRG Report – How Fictional Role Models in Entertainment Can Help Young Men Find Their Way: https://www.nrgmr.com/our-thinking/entertainment/the-lost-boys-how-fictional-role-models-can-help-young-men-find-their-way/

Common Sense Media. (2019). *The Common Sense census: Media use by tweens and teens.* Available from https://www.commonsensemedia.org/sites/default/files/research/report/8-18-census-integrated-report-final-web_0.pdf

Council on Communications and Media. (2016). 'Media use in school-aged children and adolescents'. *Pediatrics*, 138(5). doi: 10.1542/peds.2016-2592.

Coyne, S. M., Callister, M., & Robinson, T. (2010). Yes, another teen movie: Three decades of physical violence in films aimed at adolescents. *Journal of Children and Media*, 4(4), pp. 387–401. Available from doi:10.1080/17482798.2010.510006.

Equimundo and Davis Institute on Gender in Media. (2020). *If he can see it, will he be it? Representations of Masculinity in Boys Television*. Mount Saint Mary's University. Available from https://www.equimundo.org/wp-content/uploads/2020/06/GDIGM-Promundo-Masculinity-Research-2020-Final-New-Logos-combined.pdf

Plan International USA. (2018). *The state of gender equality for U.S. adolescents: Survey highlights*. Available from https://planusa-org-staging.s3.amazonaws.com/public/uploads/2021/04/state-of-gender-equality-summary-2018.pdf

UCLA Center for Scholars & Storytellers. (2025). *Tip Sheet: 10 research based insights to evolve onscreen male representation*. Available from https://www.scholarsandstorytellers.com/tipsheets

# From **Surface To Substance**: Personality Is The Future Of Engagement

**Lea Magnano**, Project Manager and UX Design Specialist, Peppy Agency

Have you ever wondered why kids today seem harder to connect with? They're no different, but their world has changed. Kids are exposed to a wider range of identities, cultures, beliefs and lifestyles than they used to be, and they care even more about how they see and express themselves. It also influences how they view brands, making them quick to pick up on anything that feels fake or superficial. Kids don't want to be addressed based on outdated stereotypes, they want something real and that speaks to who they are. That's where personality becomes a powerful angle to explore.

In addition to traditional segmentation methods, we've developed a framework that looks at kids through the lens of personality. While personality-based models already exist, they often come with one of the following issues: they're too context-specific, difficult to apply in practice, or rely on rigid categories that miss the complexity of real kids. Our approach, instead, is practical, versatile and adaptable to different uses (like product design, marketing, storytelling and edutainment), helping brands incorporate the diversity of kids' perspectives into their creative process.

## From personas to personality

Personas often lack depth and nuance. Personality, on the other hand, offers a more authentic way to represent and understand kids, but it can be challenging to translate into concrete requirements, design directions, or strategic decisions. To bridge that gap between usability and depth, we embodied our framework into five characters: Kite, Rio, Indi, Lou, and Nova. Each of these kids represents a unique blend of personality traits, grounded in psychology literature and field research.

These characters are windows into the diverse ways kids engage with the world around them. They serve as a bridge between brands and the children that companies are designing for.

Kite is resilient, outgoing, and spontaneous: a natural leader, always calm and encouraging others to embrace adventure. Rio is sociable, cooperative and a bit chaotic: brings excitement to every group game, loves to laugh, and thrives in the spotlight. Indi is inventive, reserved and free-spirited: enjoys creative, independent play and often sees the world from a unique, non-conventional perspective. Lou is detail-oriented, introverted and sensitive: thinks things through, values structure and brings care and precision to everything. Nova is curious, empathetic and adaptable: loves to observe, create and connect with friends on a deeper level.

## Why these characters work

Creating these characters wasn't done on a whim. It came from extensive research into how kids play and interact with their environment, observing children at play, interviewing experts and exploring psychological theories. We based our characters on Goldberg's Big Five theory. This widely recognized framework describes personality through five core dimensions: extraversion, agreeableness, openness to experience, conscientiousness and neuroticism. By combining varying levels of each trait, the characters reflect the complexity and diversity of children's personalities. These traits are then translated into practical and relatable characteristics for child-related contexts and given visual representations. The final result? A simple yet nuanced, research-backed way to deeply understand kids, enabling design in a way that truly speaks to who they are.

## How they can help in practice

This framework can spark ideas across multiple areas of the kids' industry, inviting all stakeholders to be more intentional: Who am I really designing for? Whose ways of thinking, interacting and engaging am I highlighting, and whose might I be overlooking?

**Toys and Games:** Imagine creating a game that speaks directly to a child's personality, instead of their gender. A child who identifies with Kite will love a toy that involves solving challenges or exploring new possibilities; whereas Lou would enjoy something slower-paced, with space to focus, sort and play with structure.

**Marketing and storytelling:** What if your brand spoke to kids on a personal level? The same product can be exciting for different reasons depending on the child. Rio might be drawn in by how your product brings people together and supports collaboration, while Indi could be more intrigued by how it supports creativity and self-expression.

**Education:** Learning becomes both more engaging and effective when it aligns with a child's personality. A kid like Nova will connect with open-ended, imaginative tasks that allow for creative thinking; children like Lou will be more likely to enjoy clear instructions and a structured learning process.

**Media:** The way content is presented to kids can also be shaped around personality. Rio will enjoy social and interactive platforms that encourage engagement with others. Nova will more likely be drawn to tools that spark creativity and offer ways to share their work with a small, trusted group, along with spaces for inspiration.

Kids today don't just want to be marketed to, they want to be seen. Whether designing toys, crafting stories, or building digital tools, personality is more than just another segmentation strategy: it's an honest and meaningful path to connect with kids. So the question is: how will your next project reflect the real, wonderful complexity of who they are?

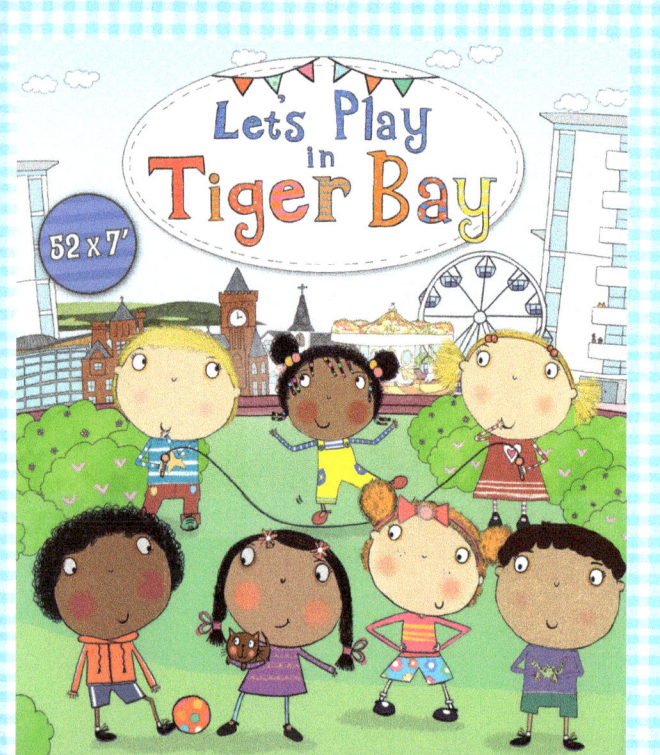

# Real-Time Magic: How AniMotion Live Is Redefining Character Engagement

 **Richard Chaney**, Creative Director, Piranha Bar

For decades, animated characters have lived inside our screens – charming us from a distance. They've made us laugh, moved us to tears, and become icons in their own right. But that relationship has traditionally been a relatively passive one-way street: we watch, they perform. At Piranha Bar, we set out to flip the script – to invite audiences into a truly live, two-way conversation with the characters they love. The result is AniMotion Live, our performance and emotion capture system powered by Unreal Engine and over a decade of innovation. And it's not just a cool trick.

This technology is already transforming how stories can be told, how kids interact with characters, and how animated IPs can stay relevant in real time. It's making animation faster, more reactive, more immersive – and infinitely more alive.

## How it works: a symphony of real-time tech

At the heart of AniMotion Live is the raw horsepower and versatility of Unreal Engine. Our custom-built character rigs take live motion data from a performer – wearing a motion and facial capture gear – and instantly translate that into a fully animated character on-screen.

All of this happens without delay. No post-production, no overnight render farms – just a real-time performance that can be broadcast to a screen, livestream or even piped into a live event. Our characters look, sound and move just like the animated personalities audiences already adore. Only now, they can respond, react and engage with fans live. We've designed AniMotion Live to be mobile and flexible. The setup can fit into an overnight bag: motion suit, headgear, gloves and some serious on-site computing power. The real magic, of course, lies in the team operating it – our talented crew of technologists, 3D artists and performers who bring the system to life.

This isn't just off-the-shelf stuff. AniMotion is the result of years of R&D at Piranha Bar – tweaking, testing, and dreaming up new ways to fuse animation innovation with immediacy.

## Bringing characters closer to their fans

We witnessed the power of AniMotion Live firsthand at Lucca Comics & Games 2024, where our animated superhero Jay from *Team Jay* met his fans – live.

And when we say 'met', we mean it. He spoke directly to kids in the crowd. He answered their questions. He laughed at their jokes. He mimicked their dance moves. The magic was palpable. That moment when a child realises the character they've watched on-screen can now see *them* – that this isn't a pre-recorded clip but a living, breathing interaction – is something extraordinary.

It's not just touching. It's transformative. In that instant, the boundary between screen and world disappears. Characters become present, responsive and – most importantly – *real*.

## Infinite possibilities for IPs

Lucca was just the beginning. AniMotion Live opens the door to a universe of possibilities for IP owners, broadcasters and brand builders.

Imagine your characters doing a live interview on TV, streaming to their followers on Twitch, or appearing on a panel at Comic-Con. What if your character could host a digital talent show, be a commentator during the Olympics or become a virtual influencer who drops hot takes in real time? With this tech, they can.

We've already had some out-there conversations about what's next – animated pundits, virtual red carpet interviews, even characters guest-hosting variety shows. (Lorne Michaels, our inbox is open.)

This isn't just about novelty. It's about connection.

Digital characters can maintain long-term relationships with audiences. They don't age. They don't fall out of favour or show up late to interviews. And with the right voice and writing behind them, they can evolve with the times, tapping into cultural moments, reacting to memes or becoming part of the zeitgeist.

## Being tactical, topical and timely

One of animation's enduring challenges is its production timelines. By the time a reference makes it through the pipeline, the moment has passed. AniMotion flips that on its head.

Once a character is AniMotion-ready, they can respond to the world *today*. They are not just reactive, but proactive – able to comment on breaking news, riff on a viral trend or step into a branded moment with perfect timing.

The key here is agility. This doesn't mean replacing long-form, high-quality linear storytelling – but adding a new layer of interactivity and responsiveness that keeps animated IPs in the conversation year-round. It's a new mindset for animation studios: be ready to speak now.

## But… what about the quality?

Let's be clear – we are animation obsessives. We live for beautiful and engaging characters, nuanced performances, and cinematic worlds. The idea of 'quick and dirty' just doesn't cut it.

But with AniMotion, you don't have to compromise quality to gain speed. We've learned how to be smart about scope. You don't need a complex crowd scene or a complicated action sequence to create impact. A one-character, tight-frame performance – well lit, well acted and well written – can be just as visually rich and emotionally resonant as any big-budget set piece.

We use the same character assets you'd see in the show. Same lighting and render quality. Just delivered through a different pipeline. The secret sauce is strategic containment: limiting the complexity of the environments and sets you build, keeping the number of characters and how they interact manageable, and making sure your performer is supported with strong direction. Do that, and you'll maintain the polish fans expect.

## Not just for live

While AniMotion shines brightest in a live context, we also use it behind the scenes to produce animated content much faster than traditional keyframe animation. Think TikToks, social shorts, promos and interactive content that needs to land now.

This allows creators and brands to populate platforms with relevant, on-trend content while maintaining character fidelity. It's ideal for when timing matters more than slow-crafted finesse.

With smart up-front planning, we're able to maintain high-production values and visual quality. In the case of the year round campaign of shorts we created for *Team Jay* by Juventus, we built bespoke sets, like our 'megatron' stage set. This allowed us to generate dynamic quick-turn around motion graphics for the epic screens surrounding our hero characters as they performed bespoke choreography to bespoke music tracks. And the full production timeline from shoot to delivery was a tiny fraction of a traditional animation project of the same duration.

Again, this doesn't replace linear animation – it complements it. Our approach is always 'form follows function'. Where long-form episodes or cinematic trailers still benefit from the depth of traditional production, AniMotion lets you cover the agile, tactical terrain.

Fans of the shows we all create will increasingly expect to encounter their beloved characters across multiple platforms and will be open to the form, style and level of interactivity (and the production values of each) they experience to be platform relevant and constantly surprising.

## The future is responsive

We believe animation is entering a new phase – one where interactivity, spontaneity and real-time presence will redefine what audiences expect from their favourite characters. The demand for bite size, 'snackable' content that's algorithm friendly and lives in the moment, will drive the evolving form of the industry's output.

AniMotion Live is our answer to that evolution. It's a performance tool and a storytelling accelerant all rolled into one.

As AI and performance capture evolve, the possibilities will only expand. Our AniMotion product isn't hardware and software specific, it's an evolving feast of technologies and we're already developing versions that incorporate AI generated elements into the pipeline.

But even as the tech grows, we never lose sight of what matters most: the connection between performer and audience. That spark of surprise when a child hears their favourite character say their name, or when a digital hero mimics their dance moves. That's where the real magic lives.

And at Piranha Bar, we're just getting started.

# Time For **BeddyByes**

**John Rice**, Co-Creator of *BeddyByes*

When Alan Shannon and I first thought of *BeddyByes*, it wasn't in some informal creative session or during a brainstorming meeting. It was around nine o'clock one evening, in the middle of a familiar struggle for both of us as parents – getting our toddlers into bed. We'd joke about our kids having energy exactly when we had none left; the reality was exhausting. But these nightly battles were a universal parenting challenge. Chats with other parents at creche pickups, family gatherings or even online confirmed that bedtime was frequently the most stressful part of their day. And research backed this up; over 60% of parents of young children describe bedtime as their primary parenting challenge. There was a gap in the market and we felt uniquely placed to address it.

Looking at existing preschool content, the absence of calming, bedtime-specific programming was striking. There were plenty of educational or fun shows, but there was very little content crafted to help parents wind their children down effectively. Parents we talked to said they relied heavily on platforms like YouTube in the hopes of finding something suitable, only to be disappointed. The gap wasn't just a missed business opportunity, but a chance to help families worldwide.

And so *BeddyByes* was born. A co-production commissioned by BBC and RTÉ, specifically created to ease children into sleep while sincerely engaging and entertaining them. Early testing involved focus groups with two–four-year-olds. We paid close attention to what held their attention whilst calming them down. Kids didn't just quietly sit through the episodes; they genuinely enjoyed the content, as did their parents. We observed children's reactions to specific story elements, animation styles, colours and music to determine what worked best. This iterative process allowed us to refine the show continuously, ensuring every element was both enjoyable and effective.

We worked closely with animators and scriptwriters to develop engaging storylines that combined gentle pacing with characters children could relate to emotionally. Consultations with child psychologists helped ensure the narratives were developmentally appropriate. Child development specialist Dr Jacqueline Harding, who emphasised how crucial good sleep is for a child's emotional, cognitive and physical development – and equally, how poor sleep can negatively impact parental wellbeing. With her guidance, we incorporated proven calming techniques into every episode, from muted colours and gentle pacing to carefully crafted background music.

Children respond best to characters and stories they find relatable and enjoyable, and so, despite this rigorous scientific grounding, the core remained storytelling. The collaboration allowed us to incorporate subtle but meaningful messages about friendship, comfort and emotional regulation, themes particularly important in early childhood development. Children respond best to characters and stories they find relatable and enjoyable.

A critical aspect of the show is routine. Each episode mirrors the comforting daily rituals familiar to toddlers and preschoolers: from playtime through mealtime, bath time and finally bedtime. The rhythm of the show reinforces what experts and parents alike understand to be crucial – predictability and structure, helping kids feel secure and calm at bedtime. We spent significant time refining these sequences to feel authentic and relatable, drawing directly from our personal experiences and extensive input from families during our focus groups.

The market quickly validated our instincts. The positive reaction from multiple broadcasters was immediate, including DR (Denmark), YLE (Finland) and SVT (Sweden). Thunderbird Entertainment came onboard early to manage international distribution and consumer products, and their expertise allows us to strategically approach licensing deals, ensuring the series is distributed effectively across diverse markets, carefully adapting marketing and distribution strategies to resonate culturally and commercially in each region.

Our licensing strategies are specifically tailored to resonate with families. Bulldog Licensing in the UK joined the team to develop a thoughtful range of consumer products complementing the series. Plush toys, storybooks, pyjamas and specialised sleep aids are just a few planned items. We are exploring detailed, research-informed product development strategies that directly respond to consumer demand, ensuring high-quality, practical items that genuinely support families.

Platforms and broadcasters globally are also recognising *BeddyByes*' unique appeal and practical utility. The series not only fills a programming gap but also serves brilliantly as an on-demand, anytime resource – not just for nightly bedtime, but also for daytime naps, long car journeys or moments when calm is simply needed. Its versatility is particularly valuable to families, providing an ideal addition to broadcaster offerings.

Looking forward, the scope for preschool programming that addresses real-world family challenges extends far beyond just bedtime. Issues like emotional regulation, developing social skills and practical life skills represent fertile ground for creators willing to listen and respond directly to family needs. Our experience with *BeddyByes* has demonstrated clearly that the best content comes from genuinely understanding and addressing the daily lives and challenges of families.

There's a real sense of excitement and pride across our entire team. We've already begun to explore potential future series and spin-offs, ensuring that the mission of supporting families extends well beyond bedtime. We're optimistic about the positive impact *BeddyByes* will have – not just on bedtime routines, but on family wellbeing and overall happiness.

*BeddyByes premiered on CBeebies and RTÉ Jr on 7th June 2025.*

# Reaching Young Audiences: Best Practice From Denmark

**Dr Eva Novrup Redvall**, Associate Professor in Film and Media Studies, University of Copenhagen

Industry professionals trying to figure out what audiovisual fiction to make for children and young audiences and then how to make it, has been one of the main interests of the research project Reaching Young Audiences (RYA) based at the University of Copenhagen (2019–2024). The project was focused on the Danish screen industries, particularly the extensive production of public service fiction targeting children and young audiences across all age-groups.

Although the project took a more national outlook than originally intended, thanks to the Covid-19 pandemic – for instance analysing how remarkably fewer Danish live action children's films were produced during the 2010s and 2020s despite the allocation of 25% of the film funding for children and young audiences, or how the Danish Broadcasting Corporation (DR) decided to cancel the popular Disney animation show on Friday nights to instead develop their own format, based on (and boosting) the national animation scene – there are still many transferable points of interest across borders and screen cultures.

The conference arranged to close the Reaching Young Audiences project in November 2023, brought together a wide range of scholars and industry professionals from around the world, and pointed to the value of meeting those with different perspectives and comparing the state of affairs across international contexts. Coming from a country with less than six million people, it is mind-blowing to think of the number of children in India and the strategies for reaching them – as discussed in the work of a scholar like Ruchi Kher Jaggi. From the Australian perspective, Anna Potter has continuously explored the developments in children's television with many pertinent points of comparison from a Danish perspective, while another collaborator of the RYA project, Jeanette Steemers, has offered valuable and transferable findings in her work on children as a particular – and often overlooked – audience in a UK as well as a global context. There is much to be learned from looking outside of one's own screen culture bubble.

There were three overall developments that we observed during our focus on Danish children's film and television production in the 2020s that might also be worthwhile to reflect upon from the UK perspective. That is: 1) a remarkable audience exploration turn; 2) a new focus on knowledge-sharing and educational initiatives; and 3) a move towards more inquiry-driven and co-creative writing and production strategies.

## The turn to working with the audience

When the RYA project started, there was little Danish research on children and their media use. This gradually emerged with the Danish Film Institute (DFI) and DR presenting new analyses on what children were in fact watching and on which platforms. As part of the RYA project, Pia Majbritt Jensen and Petar Mitric in 2023 conducted both quantitative and qualitative analyses of children's media use, pointing to e.g. a preference for international fiction once children can read subtitles and get a phone where they can pull their own content, but also to a continuous engagement with national YouTubers and social media content.

While all this data offered interesting insight into children's actual media use, a new and remarkable development was how audience research on children started being of a much more exploratory nature – wanting to know more about, for instance, what children were thinking about and dreaming of, rather than only focusing on their actual media use. A good example of this is a 2023 study of 7–18-year-olds and their lives with films, series, and social media, made for the DFI[1]. The report was presented as an attempt to serve as a resource for filmmakers to create content and for educators and policymakers to stimulate content that resonates with younger generations, arguing that knowing more about children and young people's actual behaviour, lives, emotions and thoughts is important if one wants to maintain and strengthen relevance and appeal to new generations.

This kind of research builds on a conviction that more knowledge of what it means and feels like to be a child today is needed if one is to tell engaging stories for them. Instead of mostly focusing on what children do on their phones, this demands a more qualitative dive into exploring who they are, what they are thinking about, and how one can connect to this when writing and producing new content for them.

## Knowledge-sharing and education

Findings from reports like the ones mentioned above were presented at several well-attended industry events based on trying to get new conversations going about the young audiences of today. One forum for this was the launch in 2021 of the Pan-Nordic Children's Media Conference (similar to much bigger international events, like the UK's Children's Media Conference). The conference documented a new focus on organising annual industry gatherings specifically for knowledge-sharing on children's content for practitioners working with children's screen media.

Moreover, the 2020s saw new educational and training programs emerge. Historically, there has been almost no teaching of children's fiction at the National Film School of Denmark, and no other educational institutions focusing particularly on this. This changed with the founding of the Cross-Media School of

---

1  Danish Film Institute/DFI. (2023). Close-up: A study of 7–18-year-olds and their lives with films, series, and social media. Report conducted by will&agency for the DFI. Available from https://www.dfi.dk/en/english/close/next-generation-and-their-lives-film-series-and-social-media#:~:text=This%20qualitative%20study%20explores%20the%20preferences%20and%20behaviors,as%20films%2C%20series%2C%20social%20media%20content%2C%20and%20games

Children's Fiction in 2019, which brings together writers interested in creating books, plays, film, TV, games and cross-media productions for children and young audiences, marking the first time that writers could educate themselves with a focus on audio-visual content for kids and adolescents.

Meanwhile, DR ventured into collaborations with the publicly financed national film workshops around a 'TV series school' ('Serieskolen med DR Ultra), focusing on encouraging young talent to develop potential fiction series for the DR Ultra audience of nine–14-year-olds, while also arguing that the ambition was to make new generations of filmmakers interested in children and young audiences. The structure of the school was a mix of open-to-all online lectures sharing knowledge and ideas of best practice, before the selection of a limited number of participants for bootcamps, leading to a final idea pitch for an industry panel. From the RYA perspective, it has been remarkable to see how both industry events and new educational initiatives started focusing explicitly on children as a particular audience, and it will be interesting to see the potential results of these developments.

## Inquiry-driven and co-creative strategies

In terms of what was shared and taught at these new initiatives about children and young audiences and the findings from the RYA case studies, it has been notable how the ideas of best practice in the 2020s were driven by trying to get children and young audiences closer to the production processes. In the RYA project, we discussed this as working with more inquiry-driven and co-creative strategies, where practitioners build on insights from exploratory audience research, as well as input from specific children invited to take part, during the early stages of development and writing.

The RYA project explored these strategies through analyses of 'affordable fiction' series, like the highly popular *Klassen* (*The Class*) which, in 2025, is in its 18th season, with over 1,000 episodes produced – the most episodes ever in the history of Danish television. Since its launch in 2016 *Klassen* has tried to involve the audience in many different ways, from idea generation, through feedback sessions at schools, to working with credited 'junior editors' as part of the production framework.

Many practitioners will argue that they have always looked to take young audiences seriously and listen to their voices. However, new methods involving children and young audiences have become more institutionalised and prominent – and are tied to arguments for more inclusive and collaborative approaches to achieve authenticity and relevance in the eyes of the young audiences.

*The findings presented here are discussed in more detail in* Writing and Producing for Children and Young Audiences: Cases from Danish Film and Television, *with the book also offering analyses of individual Danish case studies created for toddlers, preschool children, tweens and teens.*

*For more publications from the Reaching Young Audiences project, please visit:* https://komm.ku.dk/forskning/filmvidenskab-og-kreative-medieindustrier/rya/

# Inclusive Storytelling: Writing For Maddie + Triggs

**Jayne Kirkham**, Screenwriter

'Inclusive storytelling' is generally seen as making sure that as many perspectives, cultures and ethnicities as possible are portrayed truthfully, honestly and positively: no cheap or derogatory stereotypes, no limitations based on class, colour or creed. Inclusive storytelling then is usually understood to be about content. But writing for BBC/RTÉ's *Maddie + Triggs*, I have come to realise that inclusive storytelling also means thinking about a story's form and format. 'Show, don't tell' is one of the first things screenwriters are taught. Back in the days of lovely big cinema screens it was true that the image told you everything. In fact I was encouraged to watch movies with the sound turned down and focus purely on the 'mise-en-scene' ("Dialogue is so… bourgeois!"). But what if you can't see the flipping mise-en-scene?

Have you listened to an audio description of your favourite film? Audio description is very much an afterthought.

But what if the audio description was embedded in the text right from the get go?

I started out in experimental theatre. We had no money for elaborate sets or costumes. All we had were our bodies, a few lights and an old reel-to-reel tape recorder. We relied heavily on creating soundscapes to evoke time, place and emotions.

*Maddie + Triggs* started out as a podcast so, again, the soundscape was right at the heart of the storytelling. With a central character that has a visual impairment, and with a central message of 'taking the time to listen', adapting the show for animation meant breaking that fundamental screenwriting rule: show, don't tell!

*Maddie + Triggs* shows AND tells!

Sounds clunky. And if I'm honest, the scripts look clunky with both what is seen and what is heard written separately. But with a bit of writerly magic and brilliant teamwork, what is seen and heard blend beautifully in the finished product so that the viewer, whether they're watching or listening, can fully enjoy the story, feel for the characters and laugh at the fun.

But what's next for that viewer? Children grow up and leave behind their preschool shows. Will they find the same level of inclusive storytelling in shows for older kids? And what happens when they're adults? The visually impaired adults that I know manage with dialogue-heavy soaps ("We need to talk…") and an ever-diminishing number of radio dramas.

What if we writers and producers considered the soundscape a little more? Maybe write dialogue that subtly drops in what is being seen? Nobody wants to watch or listen to something that clunks. What is pioneered in children's often finds its way into the mainstream.

"Yes, yes, but adult drama is complex, sophisticated; we can't reduce Benedict Cumberbatch to a simple cartoon!"

OK. Then what if the audio description was not left until the end of a production, but was written by the actual episode writer? Thought about at script stage, included in the contract? There's a thought. Our screen content would then truly be more inclusive.

*Maddie and Triggs*

# ORIEL SQUARE

## Helping you design and deliver the best in educational programmes, products and services for the children you support.

 **STRATEGIC PLANNING**

 **COMMUNICATIONS**

 **IMPLEMENTATION**

 Oriel Square Limited     www.orielsquare.co.uk

  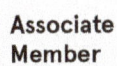 

# Are Tech Platforms Taking Over Family Life?

**Dr Sonia Livingstone**, Professor of Social Psychology, LSE and **Alexandra Evans**, Technology Policy Expert

Think of your phone – how many apps could you delete today, which do you rely on, and why? What happens if you lose your phone?

Our everyday reliance on platforms is barely more than a decade old. A long time in tech terms, but not in the evolution of the family. Already, we are talking of the platform society, of tech platforms as an infrastructure to our lives – meaning, they are ubiquitous, we rely on them every day, take them for granted, and only notice them when they break down. We have our loyalties to some, our frustrations with others, and we explore their functionality with interest, sometimes creatively, maybe gaming them to make them work for us.

We know that tech platforms are making sizeable profits. But are the changes that they bring working well for families? Meaningful relations matter to families but may not fit the business strategies or segmented markets of the platforms; are families finding a workaround or even trying to resist? In-person interaction matters to families, but is this undermined by the glowing small screen? Families think of their private life as private; does it matter to them that it's not? Is society's reliance on platforms contributing to declining trust – in institutions, businesses, even in each other?

## Platforms are big business

Platforms are big businesses – to be precise, two-sided or multi-sided markets. We, the users, are one side of the market – and they underpin our communication – think of WhatsApp, our Saturday nights (Netflix), our soundscape (Spotify), our social network (Instagram, TikTok, Snapchat). They also underpin much more – banking, health, work, education, news, shopping and travel.

How have tech platforms become among the most profitable companies in the world? That's where the other side of the market comes in. Research shows how[1] platforms track our activities, collect our personal information, profile our tastes and preferences, monetise our attention in the global data ecosystem and sort us according to our likely value to others, whether government

---

1   Erstad et al. (2024). How digital technologies become embedded in family life across generations: scoping the agenda for researching 'platformised relationality'.

or businesses, in increasingly automated and opaque ways. Yet they are not accountable to us, but to their shareholders. Our interests do not drive their business model unless it's profitable, or the government makes them.

Not only are platforms the new infrastructure for society, but they are profoundly individualistic – my phone, my Spotify playlist, my learning zone. No longer can we lend a book or magazine or borrow a game or DVD. For the platforms, the user is singular, and shared devices or passwords mess up the digital profiles they construct and monetise. For the platforms, families are also normative – they assume we cohabit in a traditional household, with parents in agreement over the purse strings and children doing as they are told.

Yet, people are social. Our relationships define us. Our mutual responsibilities connect us. Our imaginaries are jointly constructed. So, platforms are used in shared ways, including in families – a child receives her homework on Google Classroom, and her mum calls it 'our homework'. A grandfather needs help from his daughter to book a doctor's appointment on the app. People keep an eye on each other using Snap maps or Life 360. They coordinate what's for supper on WhatsApp.

And it's not all happy families. Conflict can centre on how much time on TikTok, or photos that reveal you were not where you said you'd be, or unexpected bills from a computer game. People are also diverse, and for some it may seem easier if everyone has their own account, to suit their own preferences, to enjoy with headphones on. Nor do families fit into the neat platform vision of them – in reality, they spread across households and geographies, they have secrets that data tracking should not undermine, they may include a family friend but not the in-laws. Does Alexa understand this? Should it?

Of course, the very idea of 'the family' is plural, fluid, intersectional, situated; how does that square with global platforms that valorise standardised, efficient transactions over human values, flexible meaning-making, co-constructed practices and the messy realities of everyday life? Is this a preoccupation for families, or does it go unnoticed? Are people reflexive or complicit? Are their responses generational? Or classed? How are kinship practices being made and remade in the platform society?

## The platformization of the family

A recent book of this title, published by researchers from the PlatFAMs project and Digital Child centre, proposes that families, defined as openly as possible, are being 'platformized' – meaning reshaped by platforms in ways yet to be well understood. This isn't to point to a monolithic or totalising process, but one in which families are complexly engaged in multiple ways that are also not well understood. Noticing the shifts in family life due to platformization is tricky because they happen gradually, the result of countless small decisions, often made in the moment to solve a specific problem or to meet an immediate need. A doorbell breaks and is replaced by one with a camera monitored via an app, or a parent wants to know when to put dinner on and realises he can use Find My iPhone to check his daughter's ETA, or a whole-family WhatsApp group is created in the run-up to Christmas and never gets disbanded.

For teens trying to carve their own path, something as seemingly innocuous and potentially useful as a read receipt can be a source of stress or conflict if it transforms the expectation on them to engage with wider family – extending the occasional visit, phone call or postcard into a continuous obligation to like, reply and share the daily flow of messages.

Children are not the only ones who may feel family group messages as a burden. Adult siblings may resent having to engage with self-congratulatory news and photos from their brothers or sisters or interpret their parents' effusive reaction as a subtle preference ranking or even veiled criticism. In-laws may find being pulled tightly into their relative's partner's family dynamics overwhelming. Grandparents may find it baffling that no one likes phone calls anymore, and their grandchildren live life on the small screen. Meanwhile, people who play an important role in a child's life may feel hurt when membership of a chat is drawn based on normative assumptions of who is and isn't family.

## Should society intervene in the platformization of family life?

In the UK, Ofcom's regulatory codes do not require companies to design for rights, agency or wellbeing, and companies have wide discretion on product design. This discretion is most often exercised to advance commercial interests. As a result, a feature or functionality that causes a family difficulties may not be one that they can turn off or dial down – for example, WhatsApp allows users to turn off read receipts when messaging one-to-one but not in group chats.

It is the role of policymakers and regulators to set and enforce minimum safety and privacy standards across all platforms. Irrespective of whether they are accessed by children at home, at school or when they are out and about, digital products must be age appropriate and rights-respecting by design and by default. Despite the passage of the Online Safety Act, we are a long way from this being a norm. We are even further from families being able to set parameters on platformization, including the ability to choose which aspects of a product or service they want to use and how, or which they find stressful, compulsive or burdensome in other ways.

Greater awareness of platformization is likely to lead families to question the terms on which products and services are offered and to demand greater choice and control. If these calls are ignored by tech companies, challenger brands may step in to offer more compassionate and rights-respecting alternatives or policymakers may intervene. Consulting families when diversifying market options would be a good first step.

*The ways in which the digital platforms mediate so many aspects of our commercial and personal life – and how this has begun to transform everyday family existence is explored in depth within the new book The Platformization of the Family. A version of this article was previously published in the Media@LSE Blog.*

# Preschoolers And YouTube/Kids

**Dr Jane O'Connor**, Associate Professor of Childhood Studies, Birmingham City University

YouTube/Kids is now the most watched form of media worldwide for children aged three and four; 90% of this age group in the UK accessing videos every week. The ability to choose what to watch, when to watch it and to see endless suggested videos of similar content has all but eclipsed the traditional model of carefully curated, programmed children's TV. Significantly, preschoolers are not only limited to being consumers of YouTube/Kids but, increasingly, are also producers of digital content. The number of child-user generated videos continues to grow in popularity and number, including toy unboxing, arts and crafts tutorials, pranks, baking, science experiments and 'Let's Play' videos presented by young children, also called 'micro-celebrities' or 'kid-fluencers'. Preschoolers are also an integral part of numerous YouTube families who create regular content on their children's lives and which is usually commercially sponsored.

What do three–four-year-olds like to watch? The answer is both simple and infinitely complex. Certain videos take off in an unprecedented way that is largely unpredictable. *Baby Shark* has now had 11 billion views and has become a shared cultural touchpoint for young children and their parents worldwide. More complex is the way in which YouTube/Kids allows the individual to curate their own entertainment experience, picking and choosing videos that match their current interests or aspirations. For very young children this can make the type of videos they choose very narrow – they may have an intense passion for dinosaurs for example, and choose to watch little else.

Research has found that young children like short-form, fast-paced content, they like to watch children rather than adults, they like to watch an ideal 'kid-topia' version of childhood and they like to feel connected to the presenter, who needs to be relatable and preferably a similar age to themselves. They also really like the videos they watch to be funny.

The YouTube/Kids algorithm will suggest more and more of the same sort of content, meaning that children's video 'diet' will become increasingly restricted unless the 'watch and search' history is paused in the settings using the parental controls. This is concerning as although YouTube/Kids doesn't collect children's personal data, it does collect data on what they watch, potentially building up a profile of the child as a digital content consumer from a very young age, another issue to consider in on-going debates about the growing commercialisation of childhood.

Further concerns about three–four-year-olds watching YouTube/Kids include: children copying what they see on screen and enacting inappropriate behaviours; the impact of extended non-social screen time on communication and language development; the impact of too much screen time on social skills; the physical impact of screen time on eyesight, posture and diet; and the impact of choosing and discarding endless short videos on children's attention spans and their ability to concentrate for extended periods of time on texts and lessons as they begin formal education.

A recent Korean study also found that the younger age of a child's first use of YouTube/Kids and higher usage frequency were significantly associated with increased emotional and behavioural problems. This, coupled with the results of a US study that found that durations of YouTube/Kids use among three–four-year-olds are longer among those whose parents have lower educational attainment levels and are disproportionately higher in children from lower socioeconomic status families, suggests that watching YouTube/Kids may have particular risks for children who are economically and/or socially disadvantaged.

Equally concerning is the potential of YouTube/Kids to shape the mindset of a whole generation. New research from the UAE has found that interaction with YouTube/Kids influences the aspirations and consumer behaviour of preschool-age children. According to this study, what children want to have and do and who they want to be is connected to who and what they watch on YouTube/Kids. The study also found a marked inclination towards consumerism influenced by digital content amongst three–four-year-olds. Despite YouTube/Kids having limited advertising, with ads clearly marked as such and restricted advertising on certain products, much content is sponsored and content creators build their commercial brand on attracting and keeping subscribers.

How can parents protect young children from the direct and indirect, potentially negative, outcomes of watching YouTube/Kids? Recommended strategies include limiting screen time, co-watching videos and talking to your child about what they are watching, as well as finding out about and implementing the YouTube/Kids parental controls settings.

This is good advice, but I think we may be past the point, as parents, of being able to control not just *what* our children watch, but *how* what they watch affects their developing identities and understanding of the world. The time has come for media literacy education to be a part of learning in the Early Years. I believe we need to develop age-appropriate media education for this age group in order to equip young children with the skills to make positive choices about their online viewing habits and to understand the constructed commercial nature of what they are watching on video sharing platforms.

Today's preschoolers have no choice but to grow up in a digital world. The disturbing truth is that they are being tracked and shaped as digital consumers from the moment they have their first social media profile. If we want our children to grow up with the freedom to exist and thrive beyond the screen, we need to teach them how they can enjoy the digital content they like, but to also be aware of the commercial aspects of what they are watching: to be able to differentiate between fantasy and reality in what they see portrayed online.

# AI In Childhood: **Striking The Balance** Between Innovation And Safeguarding

**Dr Amanda Gummer**, Founder and CEO, FUNdamentally Children

Artificial intelligence (AI) is revolutionising childhood experiences, from AI-powered toys and educational platforms to virtual assistants and media curation. These technologies promise personalised learning, enhanced accessibility for children with disabilities and engaging entertainment. For instance, AI tools like adaptive learning platforms have been shown to improve cognitive development by tailoring content to individual needs. However, these advancements come with significant concerns including data privacy risks, ethical dilemmas and the potential erosion of critical thinking and social skills.

The challenge for professionals lies in leveraging AI's transformative potential while protecting children's developmental needs and keeping them safe. Research highlights that AI can complement traditional education by supporting creativity, language acquisition and social interaction. Yet, over-reliance on AI risks undermining the nuanced human connections vital for emotional and social growth.

There is a complex interplay between AI's benefits and risks in child development that is worth exploring. By examining how AI influences learning, home environments and play, identifying best practices for ethical development and deployment and encouraging collaboration among educators, developers and policymakers, we can ensure AI enriches childhood without compromising its essential human elements.

## AI in learning: a double-edged sword

AI-driven educational platforms like Duolingo and Ghotit Real Writer have transformed learning by offering personalised experiences tailored to a child's progress or specific needs. These tools adapt content dynamically, fostering curiosity and motivation. For children with disabilities, such as ASD or ADHD, AI-powered interventions provide targeted support in areas such as literacy, speech development and social skills.

However, these benefits are accompanied by challenges. Excessive reliance on AI tools may stifle creativity and critical thinking by prioritising algorithmic efficiency over exploratory learning.

Automated lesson planning systems ease teacher workloads but could erode autonomy in crafting personalised lessons. Moreover, AI-based recommendations often reinforce existing knowledge patterns rather than promoting diverse perspectives.

Ethical concerns also arise regarding data privacy. Many educational applications collect sensitive information about children's learning behaviors without transparent safeguards. This raises questions about consent and the long-term implications of data misuse.

The solution lies in integrating human oversight into AI-driven education. Teachers must remain central to the educational process using AI as a tool to enhance their roles rather than replacing them. For example, while platforms like LessonUp assist in creating lesson plans, educators should refine these outputs to align with their students' unique needs. This balanced approach ensures that students develop problem-solving skills alongside digital literacy.

## AI in the home: empowering or overwhelming?

AI-powered devices like Alexa or Google Nest have become integral to family routines, assisting children with tasks such as setting reminders or answering questions. Media platforms use algorithms to recommend age-appropriate content that supports both education and entertainment. For children with additional needs, smart home technologies foster independence by helping them manage schedules or engage with interactive storytelling tools.

Despite these advantages, concerns persist about the implications of integrating AI into home life. Data privacy is a significant issue; many devices collect vast amounts of personal information without clear guidelines on usage or storage. Additionally, excessive screentime facilitated by AI-curated content can hinder physical activity and reduce opportunities for face-to-face social interactions – critical components of healthy childhood development.

Striking a balance requires active parental involvement. Families should establish clear guidelines on AI use, prioritising tools that encourage active engagement over passive consumption. For instance, interactive platforms that promote co-viewing or collaborative activities can mitigate some of the negative effects of solitary screentime. Parents should also educate children about online safety and monitor how data is shared through these devices.

By combining technology with real-world experiences – such as using storytelling apps alongside traditional reading – families can harness the benefits of AI while preserving essential developmental opportunities.

## Building AI to protect and nurture

To maximise benefits while minimising harm, responsible development of AI for children is essential. Key principles include:

- **Enhancing human interaction:** research underscores that young children learn best through social interactions and play. AI should complement rather than replace these experiences by supporting emotional growth through interactive storytelling or role-playing games.

- **Collaborating with experts:** developers must work with educators, child psychologists and specialists in early childhood development to design ethical applications tailored to children's needs.
- **Transparency in data practices:** clear policies on data collection are critical. Parents must have control over what information is gathered and how it is used to protect children's privacy rights.
- **Ethical standards:** adhering to frameworks like UNICEF's "AI for Children Toolkit" ensures alignment with global standards for child safety and well-being.

By embedding these principles into design processes, developers can create tools that nurture growth while addressing ethical concerns.

## Best-practice examples: human–AI collaboration

Effective integration of AI involves collaboration between humans and technology and there are some great examples of this being done well.

**Personalised learning:**
Duolingo adapts content dynamically but relies on teachers for contextual feedback.

**AI-assisted lesson planning:**
LessonUp streamlines content creation while allowing educators to tailor materials.

**Ethical content recommendations:**
Netflix Kids curates age-appropriate media within strict safety protocols.

**Family engagement:**
Lumo Play combines physical activity with digital interaction for shared family experiences.

## The future: a call for collaboration

As AI evolves rapidly, its role in shaping childhood demands proactive collaboration among stakeholders. Policymakers must establish adaptable frameworks addressing emerging risks while fostering innovation. Developers should prioritise ethical design practices informed by evidence-based research from educators and psychologists.

Continuous dialogue is vital to align technological advancements with developmental needs. By emphasising transparency in data use and prioritising human–AI synergy over automation alone, we can ensure that future generations benefit from enriched experiences without compromising their well-being.

## References

Childhood Trust Report (2025). *How AI toys shape young minds.*

SEFI Conference Proceedings (2023). *Generative Artificial Intelligence in Education.*

UNICEF (2024). *How is artificial intelligence reshaping early childhood development?*

Zero to Three (2024). *The Future of Artificial Intelligence in Early Childhood: Transforming the Field for Professionals and Children.*

# Rethinking Digital Safety: Inclusion, Rights And A Child's Best Interests

  **Dr Helen Sandberg**, Professor of Media and Communication Studies, Lund University and **Dr Olu Jenzen**, Professor of Media and Digital Culture, Winchester School of Art

We are witnessing a rollback of children's access to digital and social media. Public debate overwhelmingly focuses on risks and perceived harms associated with screen time and social media. Digital and social media restrictions and bans are offered as solutions. The efficiency of these policies is widely questioned, but more concerning, such measures raise questions about children's rights in the digital world. We argue that children's rights are about access to digital media as much as protection from risks. The focus should be on supporting and empowering children, not excluding them. Working towards this requires deeper and more nuanced conversations – with the children's best interest at the centre.

## Children's digital lives and rights

Young people continue to make up the highest proportion of social media users. Almost all teenagers use digital and social media daily, and 97 % of children in the UK own a phone by the age of 12. (For many children during the Covid-19 pandemic, lockdowns and school closures meant that even more of their daily lives were online.) We also see increasing use of smartphones and tablets in early childhood globally, and even if the use of social media is still limited among preschoolers, as many as 16% of Swedish children aged five–eight report regularly seeing their friends online. In other words, children, just like adults, have come to rely on digital technologies for communication, public services, education, health and wellbeing, playing, shopping, all sorts of daily activities.

Today, many children see access to digital technology as a basic need. Digital connectivity and online resources are also vital to children in times of crisis or to handle uncertainty. The UN Convention on the Rights of the Child supports the right of a child to have access to digital technologies, social media and online communities for communication and other activities. The Convention's 'General Comment 25' emphasises that even though most digital environments were not originally made for children, they are crucial to them now and therefore the best interests of every child should be prioritised across 'the provision, regulation, design, management and use of the digital environment'[1].

---

1    General Comment 25 (2021) is available from the UN Digital Library: https://digitallibrary.un.org/record/3906061

## New developments and global trends

Governments and policymakers have advocated for implementing new age restrictions and other restrictive measures, such as restricting children's use of smartphones. As scholars with longstanding expertise in children and digital media, we find these developments worrisome.

Most social media platforms require users to be 13 or older to have a user account. However, age limits are regulated differently across different countries and, recently, we have seen some rollback of younger teenagers' access to social media, such as Australia's social media ban for under 16-year-olds; France's lobbying for an EU-wide policy requiring parental authorisation for children under 15 to use a social network service; a similar call for a 15+ age limit by Denmark's Prime Minister; Instagram's introduction of a 'teen' (aka parental control) version in the UK; and other countries implementing restrictions aimed at limiting social media use for teenagers under 16.

Accountability is paramount, and making social media platforms, apps and other online services more responsible for user safety is important. Policies such as the UK's Online Safety Act (2023) aimed at strengthening children's rights in online environments concerning datafication, privacy and consent are positive developments. However, debates on the 'banning of' social media or new restrictions to children's digital access focus mostly on risks and negative aspects, overlooking positive and beneficial ones and arguing for restrictions in the name of protection, curtailing rather than improving children's digital worlds.

> "We need research designed to capture the richness and diversity of children's experiences, ... that pays attention to children's perspectives."

The research available to policymakers is mainly made up of surveys focussing on health risks. This is a too narrow approach if we want to understand how children engage with digital and social media in their everyday lives. Evidence suggests that simplistic approaches to limiting children's time spent on screen-based media are ineffective. To avoid oversimplifying a complex reality, we need research designed to capture the richness and diversity of children's experiences. To authentically strengthen children's rights, we need research that pays attention to children's perspectives.

Photo by Vitaliy Zalishchyker on Unsplash

## Bans conflict with children's rights

However, more importantly, not enough consideration has been given to the impact of restrictions, such as social media rollbacks, on groups of marginalised children for whom digital connections and internet-based platforms are vital. For example, the potentially negative impact of restrictive approaches on refugee and migrant children, LGBTQ+ children, and children with disabilities, as well as other marginalised groups of children, is rarely noted in policy and public discourse. Overall, not enough attention has been given to the role of digital and social media in children's political engagement and civic participation, which may be seriously impacted following rollback measures. This is a critical concern as children use social media to engage – as citizens – with a wide range of topics that they care about, often local, sometimes global, and, in doing so, not only practice their political voice, but enact their right to be heard.

Researchers and professionals must take care to better understand the role of digital and social media in children's everyday lives, and to speak back to simplistic calls to ban children from using these technologies. Banning might be considered a quick fix for politicians. However, it has long-term effects on children's lives. Regarding the proposed ban for under-16s in Australia, Human Rights Law Professor Sarah Joseph argues that such a ban would not only 'disrupt the flow of political communication to and from children', but also 'deprive us all of children's political voices on social media'. This means we stand to lose out on children's activism on issues that concern them and their contribution to debates on key global challenges such as climate change.

In particular, it is important to consider the need of groups of children who experience high levels of inequalities and discrimination or whose rights are being denied to have access to the public sphere for information, advocacy and breaking out of isolation. Across our research with LGBTQ+ teenagers over the years, we find many testimonials of how access to digital and social media is vital. For example, many children described how, during the Covid-19 pandemic, staying connected online helped them cope with lockdown in an unsupportive and sometimes unsafe home environment.

## Children as rights holders

The focus must be on supporting and empowering children, not excluding them. Working towards this requires deeper and more nuanced conversations centring the best interest of children, not performative 'quick fix' solutions. In debates about access to digital environments, including social media, children should be regarded as rights holders: children's competency and agency should be respected, and their right to have a say in matters that affect them be recognised. Following this, efforts should be made to find ways in which children can be involved in policy and research.

As researchers and professionals across children's media, education and youth work, we should use our insights into how diverse children and their everyday digital lives are to challenge reductive approaches. We should advocate for all children's rights in these matters, support child participation and actively involve a much more diverse range of children.

# CONNECTING BRANDS
# WITH KIDS AND FAMILIES
## SINCE 1999

**RESEARCH**
Full service agency and Kids Trends data

**METAVERSE**
We create award winning Roblox and Fortnite experiences

**APPS & EDTECH**
Our games are played by millions of kids and families

Dubit.io

hello@dubit.io

# Remembering Julie Stevens

1936–2024

Actress and singer, Julie Stevens, died on the 5th December 2024, aged 87. She had bravely battled Parkinson's for three years.

To many generations of preschool children, she was one of the all-time great *Play School* presenters (595 programmes from 1964–1978 – only two presenters, Carol Chell and Brian Cant, presented more). She is fondly remembered for her zany humour and lovely singing voice.

Her other children's TV credits were: Storyteller on *Bizzy Lizzy* (BBC One 1967), *Play School*'s spin-off show *Play Away* (40 editions from 1971–1979), *Cabbages and Kings* (BBC One, 1972 and 1974), *All Star Record Breakers* (BBC One, 1974–1980) and *Star Turn* (BBC One, 1976–1977).

Julie also provided vocals for the BBC Schools' programme *Look and Read* (1981–1988).

She was born Julie Bullas on the 20th December 1936 and later changed her surname, and as she had an Uncle Stevenson, became Julie Stevens.

She worked as a nurse at the Manchester Royal Infirmary and auditioned for and appeared in the ITV North Region talent show from Manchester, called *Bid for Fame*. Although she didn't win the talent contest, she was given a seven-year contract with ABC Television and appeared in a range of programmes: "In 1962, following a seven-month Equity strike, I lost my contract. I had been earning £15 a week and would have had to have been paid £35 a week whether I had worked or not – I was therefore deemed too expensive and bye, bye! That was on the Tuesday and on the Friday I auditioned and got six episodes starring as Venus Smith in *The Avengers* for ABC (1962–1963). I was paid considerably more than if I had been under my original contract!"

She made a fleeting appearance as Cleopatra's servant Gloria in *Carry on Cleo* (1964).

She knew lifelong friend, Canadian Rick Jones, from working together at Library Theatre in Manchester and he suggested Julie to *Play School*'s creator Joy Whitby. She was due to give birth to her son, so didn't appear until the sixth week. As she explained to me: "I don't recall much of that very first week with Rick, apart from the pain I was still encountering from the stitches and the fact that I had to sit on the edge of everything!"

Julie always helped new male presenters settle in, including Colin Jeavons and Fred Harris. As a young viewer, if it was Julie's week, you knew you would have lots of fun with her. I always remember her with Lionel Morton, when she had Julie's tea shop with the toys and she shook a jelly madly!

She appeared in many notable editions of *Play School*, including the 2nd, 3rd, 5th and 10th anniversaries and the 1,000th edition with Colin Jeavons (19th February 1968).

*The 5th anniversary of Play School, with Rick Jones and Julie*

Julie presented the 500th edition with Brian Cant on 21st March 1966. It had a royal visit when HRH Prince Andrew (aged six) and Viscount David Linley (aged four) came to Riverside Studios with six friends and their governess, Nanny Catherine Peebles. They spent the afternoon looking round and playing on the set. She returned with fellow former presenters, on *Twenty Five Minutes Peace*, to celebrate the 15th anniversary of *Play School* (BBC Two, April 1979).

Her TV acting credits were: *Z Cars* (BBC TV, 1963), *Girls about Town* (ATV, 1970–1971),

*The Dick Emery Show* (BBC One, 1973) and *Holby City* (BBC One, 2001). She presented the afternoon magazine programme *Not for Women Only* (TVS, 1982) and *All Kinds of Everything* with Fred Dinenage and Marian Davies (HTV West, 1982) and appeared in an advert for Mellow Bird's Coffee.

I first met Julie in 1989, when she was working for Sir Harry Secombe.

Julie became a great supporter of the memory and history of *Play School*. 30 years after her departure from Children's BBC, she attended my book launch at BAFTA in 2010 and joined many former colleagues for the 50th anniversary reunion of *Play School*'s first edition at its original home, Riverside Studios, in May 2014.

She lived in France for many years and returned to the UK in 2017 to live near her daughter, Rachel New, and grandchildren, in Birmingham. Rachel told me that her years on Children's BBC were the happiest of her life and she loved knowing that she had such an impact on children's lives and was remembered so fondly.

Julie was married to fellow actor and *Play School* presenter John White (1962–1975). Her second marriage was to actor/theatre director Michael Hucks (1981–2001).

I was always a fan and was honoured that she looked at me as a friend through our shared love of *Play School*.

**Paul R Jackson**, Author, *Here's a House – A Celebration of Play School*

# Remembering **Peter Murphy**

1111–1111

Peter Murphy, who died on 30th December 2024, dedicated his whole career to working with and for children, first in theatre and then in television. As well as being one of the founders of Nottingham's influential Television Workshop, he also kick-started the success of Ant and Dec.

In a tribute to him, Declan Donnelly wrote: "When we left *Byker Grove* and were looking at what we were going to do next, Peter saw something in Ant and me, and our friendship, and championed us to anyone who would listen. I don't think it's a stretch to say that at the time, he believed in us more than we did. He was the driving force behind *The Ant and Dec Show* being commissioned by the BBC and was integral to launching us on the TV path we took in our careers."

*The Ant and Dec Show* went on to win a BAFTA award for best children's TV programme in 1996, as did an earlier show that emerged from The Television Workshop, *Your Mother Wouldn't Like It*, which was cast totally from members of the Workshop and based on their improvisations.

Peter began his career in the mid 1970s as an actor with the Breconshire Theatre Company, before joining the Cockpit Theatre, London as an actor-teacher in 1974. He also worked as head of education at the Young Vic, under the direction of Michael Bogdanov in the late 1970s.

In the 80s Peter became a trainee children's producer before joining Central Independent Television, working alongside Lewis Rudd, Controller of Children's and Young People's Television. Together they hatched the 'Anna Scher of the Midlands', setting up a drama workshop for kids and thereby creating a casting pool for its output. In 1988, he moved to HTV as Head of Children's Programmes, then on to Zenith Productions, where he spotted the potential of Ant and Dec.

Peter's superpower was spotting young talent. Actors who started out at the TV Workshop include Samantha Morton, Vicki McClure, Jack O'Connell, Joe Dempsie and Bella Ramsey,to name but a few. Alison Rashley, who now runs the Workshop, said: "So many of us from that time owe so much to Peter for letting us believe there was a place for us in this industry".

**Sue Nott**, Freelance Executive Producer and Consultant

# Contributors

### Rebecca Atkinson

Rebecca Atkinson is a Writer, Creator and Executive Producer working across children's industries, both commercial and non-profit. She is a specialist in storytelling, play theory, innovation and inclusion by design.

Rebecca is the Creator, EP and writer of Mixmups, the magical award winning pre-school stop-motion series for Milkshake! C5, produced by Mackinnnon and Saunders, and the innovator and EP of the Ultra Access™ service powered by Stornaway.

Rebecca is currently working on an upcoming series of industry-first paper engineered novelty books for an international publisher.

### Ivan Barroso

Ivan Barroso was born in 1980 in Lisbon. He is currently an Assistant Professor at Universidade Lusófona, teaching in the BSc in Videojogos programme, and at the Polytechnic Institute of Leiria, in the BSc in Games and Multimedia programme. His academic research focuses on game history and game studies. Barroso is the author of three published books: *História dos Videojogos* (2012), *Service Games: The Rise and Fall of SEGA* (2014), and *Revolução Interactiva* (2018). He is certified in Rational Game Design by Ubisoft and serves as the Lead PlayStation® First Project Manager at GameNest® Lisbon. Most recently, he served as the Project Manager and Game Designer for *Alentejo: Tinto's Law©*, developed by Loading Studios for the Game Boy, PC, and mobile platforms.

### Professor Rachael Bedford

Rachel is Professor of Biological and Experimental Psychology at the Queen Mary University of London and part of the Animating Minds consortium.

### Dr Sergio Benini

Sergio is Associate Professor of Telecommunications at the Department of Information Engineering, University of Brescia, and part of the Animating Minds consortium.

### Dr Cassie Brummit

Cassie Brummitt is Assistant Professor in Film and Television at the University of Nottingham. Her research revolves around industry studies of contemporary film and television. She is the author of *From Harry Potter to the Wizarding World: The Transfiguration of a Franchise* (Edinburgh University Press, 2025). She is engaged in projects that address challenges facing the cinema exhibition sector in the East Midlands.

### Richard Chaney

Richard Chaney is Creative Director at Piranha Bar, a hybrid creative studio that merges storytelling, character design, and technology to create unforgettable animated experiences. Their AniMotion Live product represents the cutting edge of real-time character performance for children's media, branded entertainment and beyond.

### Dr Diane Charlesworth

Diane Charlesworth was for 25 years an academic in film and television studies at the University of Lincoln, who taught a range of screen studies topics, including a module on children's film and television. She is currently an independent scholar and senior Honorary Fellow of the University of Lincoln, researching and publishing on BBC post-war children's television.

### Greg Childs OBE

Greg Childs OBE is Director of the Children's Media Foundation.

Greg worked for over 25 years at the BBC, mainly as a director, producer and executive producer of children's programmes. He created the first Children's BBC websites and, as Head of Children's Digital, developed and launched the children's channels, CBBC and CBeebies. Greg left the BBC in 2004 and went on to advise producers on digital, interactive and cross-platform strategies, and broadcasters on channel launches, digital futures and operational management. He was in the launch teams for Teachers TV and the CITV Channel in the UK, and was advisor to the Al Jazeera Children's Channel for three years. He also consulted with the European Broadcasting Union on their Children's and Youth strategy.

In his role as Editorial Director of the Children's Media Conference (CMC), Greg has grown this annual event into a gathering of 1,000+ delegates, with over 200 speakers, while CMC also hosts the British delegation to the important Kidscreen market in the USA. Up to 2019, Greg also spent 15 years as one of the Heads of Study for the German Akademie für Kindermedien.

Greg was awarded an OBE in the 2022 New Year Honours List for services to exports and the children's media sector.

### Sam Clough

Sam is the Global Head of Strategic Research and Insights at SuperAwesome, an award-winning technology company that powers the youth digital ecosystem, helping brands to meet their audience where they are.

She is an expert on youth audiences, having spent 30 years researching kids, teens and families. At SuperAwesome, she leads the insights team, empowering the business to dig deeper and build a nuanced understanding of evolving trends.

Sam is a passionate advocate for her audience, giving a voice to an often overlooked group. Her groundbreaking research, which spans children from preschool age through adulthood, has been pivotal in establishing SuperAwesome as the leading expert and thought leader in the youth digital space.

## Frank Cottrell-Boyce

Award-winning author and screenwriter, Frank Cottrell-Boyce, is the Waterstones Children's Laureate 2024–2026.

He is the author of *Sputnik's Guide to Life on Earth*, *The Astounding Broccoli Boy*, *Cosmic*, *Framed* and *Millions*, the last of which was a New York Times bestseller and was made into a movie by Oscar-winning director Danny Boyle.

His books have won or been nominated for numerous awards, including the Carnegie Medal, the Guardian Children's Fiction Prize, and the Whitbread Children's Book Award. Frank is also a screenwriter, having penned the scripts for a number of feature films including *24 Hour Party People* and *Millions* as well as the opening ceremony of the 2012 London Olympics. He lives in Liverpool with his family.

## Sarah Cox

Sarah Cox sits on the Board of Directors at Aardman and leads the Development and Creative Pillar. In her role as Chief Creative Director she is responsible for shaping the creative strategy of the studio and the development slate. She has brought a range of new projects to the Aardman roster that include the Oscar nominated stop frame musical *Robin Robin* and Aardman's first CG series *Lloyd of the Flies* and developed the *Morph* spin off preschool show *The Very Small Creatures* which is now in its third season. Her Executive Producer credits include two Emmy winning *Shaun the Sheep* productions and the Oscar-nominated and BAFTA-winning *Wallace & Gromit: Vengeance Most Fowl*. She has initiated at Aardman, a slate of animated IP collaborations that include productions for Lucasfilm and Pokémon and in development with Mattel on *Pingu*.

## Jackie Edwards

Jackie is a passionate advocate for public service television and until very recently, was living her dream job as the Head of the British Film Institute's Young Audiences Content Fund, responsible for the implementation of this game-changing UK Government initiative to stimulate the provision of public service content for audiences of 0–18.

This hugely successful three-year pilot awarded £44.1M of funding supporting 61 brand new commissions for UK children and teens and funded the development of a further 160 new projects, over 9% of which have already been commissioned. Shows supported range from *Milo* and *The World According to Grandpa* through to *Big Boys* and *Don't Hug Me I'm Scared*. The fund has been a powerful lever in stimulating a sector in market failure.

Jackie joined the BFI in 2019 from BBC Children's where she was the Head of Acquisitions and Independent Animation, responsible for pre-buying and acquiring live-action and animated programming for CBeebies, CBBC and iPlayer. She joined the BBC in 2008 as Content Manager and Executive Producer.

Jackie worked on a wide range of programming including *Rastamouse*, *Hey Duggee*, *Octonauts*, *Boy Girl Dog Cat Mouse Cheese*, *Clangers*, *Poppies* and *The Next Step*.

Prior to the BBC, Jackie was an award-winning producer in the independent sector for 14 years, developing, financing and producing specials and series for young audiences.

## Dr Claire Essex

Claire is a Postdoctoral Research Fellow at the Creative Computing Institute, University of Arts London, and part of the Animating Minds consortium.

## Professor Elizabeth Evans

Elizabeth Evans is Professor of Screen Cultures at the University of Nottingham. Her research explores screen technologies, audiences and industries. She is the author of *Transmedia Television: Audiences, New Media and Daily Life* (Routledge, 2011), *Understanding Engagement in Transmedia Culture* (Routledge, 2020) and *The Enchanting Kinora: Domesticating Moving Images in Edwardian Britain* (BFI, 2025). She has worked with a number of industry partners including cinemas across the East Midlands, artist collection Urban Angel and Warner Bros.

## Alexandra Evans

Alexandra's work focuses on the impact of technology on children and childhood. She develops product and policy responses to the challenges children face and has played a key role in developing age-appropriate design standards. Her perspective has been shaped by her experience working as a content regulator (BBFC), a child online safety advocate (5Rights Foundation) and within a global tech company (TikTok). Before focusing on childhood and digital, Alexandra was a solicitor (Mishcon de Reya) where she advised on discrimination and human rights, reputation management and education law.

## Maxine Fox

Maxine is a specialist in conducting research with younger audiences and families, with over 15 years' working within the industry. Maxine has worked across a diverse range of categories, fusing qualitative and quantitative research into one strong narrative, giving the assurance to brands that budgets are being spent in the right way and strategies are informed rather than predicted. As a Certified Market Research Member (CMRS), Maxine mentors' other researchers and provides advice on best practice within kids and youth research.

## Professor Mick Grierson

Mick is Professor of Computing at the Creative Computing Institute, University of Arts London, and part of the Animating Minds consortium.

## Dr Amanda Gummer

The Good Play Guide was founded by child development expert Dr Amanda Gummer in 2012. Created to provide an independent, expert accreditation service for children's products, the guide provides a trusted resource for parents and gift-givers to find truly good toys, apps and much more.

Amanda has a PhD in Neuropsychology, the Postgraduate Certificate in Higher Education and over 20 years' experience working with children and families.

Having worked in children's industries for many years, Amanda is now widely considered as the UK's go-to expert on play, toys and child development. She can regularly be seen in the media, including BBC News, Sky News, the *Daily Mail* and many more, offering advice on news stories and issues surrounding children, families and child development.

## Anna Home OBE

Anna is Chair of the CMF Board and a founder Lifetime Patron of the organisation.

Anna joined BBC radio in 1960 and started in Children's Television in 1964 where she worked as a researcher, then Director, Producer and Executive Producer, latterly specialising in Children's Drama. She started *Grange Hill*, the controversial school series. From 1981–1986 she worked at the ITV company TVS where she was Deputy Director of Programmes. In 1986 she returned to the BBC as Head of Children's programmes responsible for all children's output. She revived the Sunday teatime classic dramas and one of her last decisions before retiring was to commission *Teletubbies*.

After retiring from the BBC, Anna was Chief Executive of the Children's Film & Television Foundation until it merged into CMF in 2012.

Anna has won many awards including a BAFTA lifetime achievement award. She was the first chair of the BAFTA Children's Committee, has chaired both the EBU Children's and Youth Working Group and the Prix Jeunesse International Advisory Board. Anna was the Chair of the Save Kids' TV Campaign and the Showcomotion Children's Media Conference Advisory Committee.

## Paul R Jackson

Paul R Jackson grew up watching *Play School* in the late 1960s. He became the programmes archivist, meeting many of the presenters and production teams over the years. He is the author of the two-volume *Here's A House – A Celebration of Play School* (2010). He helped organize the 50th anniversary reunion in 2014 at Riverside Studios.

From 1984, Paul worked for BBC and ITV/Carlton TV, mostly in the Duty Office. Since 1997, he has been a freelance stage manager/talent liaison on over 100 live award shows.

He continues his archive work for the TV Room website – https://showreel.thetvroom.com

## Professor Olu Jenzen

Olu Jenzen is a Media and Digital Culture scholar based at the University of Southampton, UK. She has research expertise in digital activism and LGBTQ+ youth cultures, specialising in participatory research with young people. Jenzen currently leads an AHRC-funded project on how community belonging can improve liveability, build collective resilience, and support trans and gender diverse young people's wellbeing. She is co-editor of *The Aesthetics of Global Protest* (AUP 2020) and has published in journals such as *Convergence*; *Feminist Media Studies*; *International Journal of Health Services*; *Social Movement Studies* and *Youth*.

## Karolina Kaminska

Karolina Kaminska has worked as a journalist for over a decade, specialising primarily in business news across sectors from retail to media. She has been reporting exclusively on the TV and content industries since 2019, when she joined C21Media as a senior reporter. Karolina became editor of C21's children's brand, C21Kids, in 2021.

## Hannie Kirkham

Hannie is Research and Strategy Manager for Oriel Square, an education consultancy specialising in teaching and learning materials. Hannie leads strategy, market research and product development alongside thought leadership publications and events, and customer insights projects. She has over ten years experience in educational publishing for print and digital media in the UK and internationally, and is a primary school governor. Hannie also has an interest in the intersection between children's education and entertainment and has worked with the Children's Media Conference as Newsletter Editor, Blogger and Producer, as well as Co-Editor the Children's Media Yearbook.

## Jayne Kirkham

With over 30 years' experience working with, and writing for children and young people, Jayne has worked on a wide range of theatre, film, TV, radio and online scripts, ranging in size from small conservation films in Africa to international feature films and, most recently, RTÉ/BBC's *Maddie + Triggs*. She taught at the Northern Film School for 14 years and is a member of the board of directors of the Children's Media Foundation. She is currently working as a development consultant while in her free time, inventing a new literary subgenre of weird fiction, which, until she can coin a shorter name, she calls Crazy-Gothic-Waterwheelpunk. See her website https://jaynekirkham.com for more information.

### David Kleeman

Strategist, analyst, author, speaker, connector, David Kleeman has led the children's media industry in developing sustainable, child-friendly practices for more than three decades. He began this work as president of the American Center for Children and Media and is now Senior Vice President of Global Trends for Dubit, a strategy/research consultancy and games studio.

When he began this work, 'children's media' meant television. Today, he is fascinated by, and passionate about, kids' wide range of possibilities for entertainment, engagement, play and learning. David uses research, insights and experience to show that much may change, but children's developmental path and needs remain constant.

David is advisory board chair to the international children's TV festival PRIX JEUNESSE, on the board of the Children's Media Association and the Advisory Board of the Joan Ganz Cooney Center. In 2023, he was in the inaugural class of Children's and Family Emmys Silver Circle inductees, for 25+ years of service.

### Professor Sonia Livingstone OBE

Sonia Livingstone is Professor of Social Psychology in the Department of Media and Communications at LSE. Taking a comparative, critical and contextual approach, her research examines how the changing conditions of mediation are reshaping everyday practices and possibilities for action. She has published twenty books on media audiences, media literacy and media regulation, with a particular focus on the opportunities and risks of digital media use in the everyday lives of children and young people.

### Baroness Anne Longfield

Baroness Anne Longfield is a passionate champion for children, influencing national debate and policy to improve their lives, particularly the most vulnerable, for over three decades. She previously established and chaired the Commission on Young Lives.

From March 2015 to February 2021, she served as Children's Commissioner for England. Anne has also led a national children's charity, contributed to the delivery of the Sure Start programme in the No 10 Strategy Unit. Currently, she is the Independent Chair of the NHS Children and Young People Learning Disability and Autism Board, a non-executive director of the Bradford Children and Family Trust, and a board member of the Northern Powerhouse Partnership, having previously served on the Times Education Commission.

### Lea Magnano

Lea Magnano is a Designer and Play Consultant focused on kids' wellbeing social and emotional learning. With a background in UX and Interaction Design, she helps brands and organizations create playful and meaningful experiences that support children's development and self-expression. She currently works at Peppy Agency, where she leads workshops and projects that bridge strategy, creativity, and child-centered design.

### Richard Marson

After graduating from the University of Durham, Richard joined the BBC, where he trained as a director and producer, working on programmes like *Record Breakers* and *Tomorrow's World*, developing a vocation in working for young audiences. He spent a year producing and directing *Disney Adventures* and *Disney Club*, and also directed Channel 4's *The Big Breakfast*. He returned to the BBC in 1997 to join *Blue Peter*, where he remained for a decade, spending four years as the programme's Editor. During this time, he won a BAFTA, was nominated for an RTS award and was invited to Buckingham Palace to present a copy of his book celebrating the show's 50th anniversary to the late Queen Elizabeth II.

In more recent years, he was Executive Producer for nine series of CBBC's fly-on-the-wall documentary series *Our School*, as well as programmes for BBC2, BBC3 and Sky One.

He is the author of several books, including *Totally Tasteless: The Life of John Nathan-Turner, Drama and Delight: The Life of Verity Lambert*, and *Biddy Baxter: The Woman Who Made Blue Peter*, which was a Daily Mail Book of the Week. *A Box of Delights*, his history of the heyday of BBC children's programmes, is forthcoming.

### Gráinne McGuinness

Gráinne McGuinness is an award winning creator of standout stories for young children that encourage them to see the world in different ways. As Creative Director at Paper Owl Films, Gráinne leads the development of ambitious content for international audiences.

Creator of *Pablo* for CBeebies and RTÉJr., the series is celebrated all over the world for its timely portrayal of a smart little autistic character. She is currently developing Series 3, with a colourful musical theatre show in the works and a series of ladybird books with Penguin Random House.

Recent projects include *Sol*, a special about a young boy on a quest to bring the light back to the world after the death of his beloved grandmother and *Ladybird & Bee*, a first-hand view of nature from two little friends in Wild Meadow, and *Happy the Hoglet*. Credits also include two series of preschool cookery show *Bia Linn* for TG4 & 8-12s cookery with *Ár mBia Ár Slí* for RTÉJr.

### Alisa Musatova

Alisa is a Research Assistant at the Creative Computing Institute, University of Arts London, and part of the Animating Minds consortium.

### Sue Nott

Sue is a freelance Executive Producer and Consultant, specialising in children's and family drama. Recent credits include *The Lodge* (Disney), *Jamie Johnson* (CBBC), *The Worst Witch* (CBBC/Netflix/ZDF) and *Biff & Chip* (CBeebies).

Her producer credits in children's television cover all genres from drama and comedy to documentary and magazine, including BAFTA award winners such as *Coping With Relatives* and *The Ant and Dec Show*. For 18 years she was at the BBC, first as an Executive Producer in Education Production and then as Head of Education for BBC Children's, where she exec'd a wide range of schools programmes from hard-hitting teen drama to preschool puppet shows, and was responsible for the birth of *Tracy Beaker*. Sue was then part of the CBBC commissioning team for nine years, with responsibility for all independently produced drama including *Eve*, *So Awkward*, *Hank Zipzer*, *Roy and Rocket's Island*, as well as helping to establish ground-breaking cross platform dramas *Dixi* and *Secret Life of Boys*.

## Alex Oakley

Alex is a Research Intern at the Queen Mary University of London, and part of the Animating Minds consortium.

## Dr Jane O'Connor

Jane is an Associate Professor of Childhood Studies at Birmingham City University and Deputy Director of the Centre for the Study of Practice and Culture in Education (CSPACE). Jane is an expert in child celebrities and the history of child stars. She is author of *The Cultural Significance of the Child Star* (Routledge, 2012) and co-editor of *Childhood and Celebrity* (Routledge, 2017). Jane's other research interests include children's use of digital technology, representations of children in the media and teacher educators use of digital technology. Jane is currently leading two international British Council funded projects supporting digital transformations in Vietnamese Higher Education.

Email: Jane.O'Connor@bcu.ac.uk

X: @JaneOConnor100

## Aldrich Pan

Aldrich is Research Fellow for the Creative Computing Institute at the University of Arts London, and part of the Animating Minds consortium.

## Dr Paola Pinti

Paola is Senior Research Laboratory Developer at the Center for Brain and Cognitive Development, Birkbeck University of London, and part of the Animating Minds consortium.

## Dr Eva Novrup Redvall

Eva Redvall is Associate Professor and Head of Section for Film Studies and Creative Media Industries at the University of Copenhagen. Her research focuses on screenwriting and production, most recently as Principal Investigator of the research project Reaching Young Audiences (funded by Independent Research Fond Denmark) with findings published in the anthology *Audiovisual Content for Children and Young Audiences* in Scandinavia and the monograph *Writing and Producing for Children and Young Audiences*. Besides her academic work, she has been a film critic for the newspaper Information since 1999 and served on the board of the Danish Film Institute 2018–2025.

## John Rice

John Rice is CEO & Co-Founder of JAM Media. In his role, he sets down the vision, strategy and subsequent implementation program for the company, whilst also executive producing many of JAM's productions. John is currently Executive Producer on *BeddyByes* recently executive produced *Becca's Bunch* for Nickelodeon and *Little Roy* for BBC, a spin off of *Roy* which has won numerous international awards including a BAFTA, a Royal Television Society Award and a Kidscreen Award.

John has directed the award-winning short film *Escape* and co-produced the short film *Badly Drawn Roy*, and is also the Co-Founder of the Animation Dingle Festival. Prior to JAM Media, he held senior roles with a variety of international animation studios, including FOX Animation and MTV in the USA. John holds a Masters in Multi-Media from Trinity College, Dublin, and is currently serving on the board of Europe's Cartoon Media.

## Professor Helena Sandberg

Helena Sandberg, from the Department of Communication at Lund University, Sweden, is an internationally recognised scholar in digital communication with expertise in children's digital media, digital culture and online marketing. Sandberg's research has focused on children and online advertising, sponsored content and merchandising and engagement with apps and commercial platforms. More recently, through the DIGIKIDS project, she investigates the introduction of digital screen technology and digital media practices in early childhood (0–3 years) and modern family life. Her work is published in e.g, *Contemporary Issues in Early Childhood*, *Children & Society*, and *Journal of Early Childhood Literacy*.

## Dr Mattia Savardi

Mattia is Postdoctoral Research Fellow at the Department of Information Engineering, University of Brescia, and part of the Animating Minds consortium.

## Rebekkah Silver

Rebekkah is a graphic designer and owner of Argentum Design. Rebekkah's 10 years of experience managing and delivering creative projects spans education, publishing, academia, live events, and digital and print media. She is a specialist in creative problem-solving, complex project management and accessibility, and has worked for many major brands, including Oxford University Press, National Trust, *The Sunday Times* and QA. Rebekkah has been lead designer on the Children's Media Yearbook since 2022.

Rebekkah is available for commissioning and is contactable at rebekkah@argentumdesign.co.uk.

### Laura Sinclair

Laura is a Doctoral Researcher at Cardiff University's School of Journalism, Media and Culture researching gender representation on preschool public service broadcast television. Laura has published research that questions the current state of representation and how young audiences experience seeing themselves on screen. Laura is an Associate Fellow of the Higher Education Academy, Guest Lecturer, Co-Editor of the Children's Media Yearbook, and is currently working on the UKRI Strength and Places Fund research and development programme, Media Cymru.

### Professor Tim Smith

Tim J Smith BSc PhD is Professor of Cognitive Data Science in the Creative Computing Institute, University of the Arts London and head of the Cognition in Naturalistic Environments (CINE) Lab. He applies empirical Cognitive and Developmental Psychology methods to questions of Media Cognition and has published widely on the subject both in *Psychology* and *Media* journals. His research has informed media practices through collaborations with Dreamworks Animation, BBC, Channel 4, and the Academy of Motion Picture Arts and Sciences.

### Dr Carla Sousa

Carla Sousa has a PhD in Communication Sciences, a Master's Degree in Clinical and Health Psychology, and a Bachelor's Degree in Psychology. Her main research targets are directed toward media studies, with a particular focus on games, inclusion, behavior, learning and human diversity. In Lusófona University (Portugal), Carla is part of the Centre for Research in Applied Communication, Culture, and New Technologies (CICANT) and is an assistant professor in the Bachelor's Degrees in Videogames and Psychology. Carla has been part of several national and internationally funded projects and scientific networks. Since 2022, Carla has been an individual ambassador for the non-profit Women in Games and, since 2023, a member of the advisory board of ECREA. Currently, she also serves as the president of Sociedade Portuguesa de Ciências dos Videojogos (SPCV).

### Jeremy Swan

Jeremey Swan began his career as a child actor in the Dublin Gate Theatre. After working as a theatre stage manager and scenic artist he joined the Irish film industry at Ardmore Studios as an Assistant Director, where he worked on *The Spy Who Came in from the Cold*, starring Richard Burton.

From Irish television's RTÉ he moved to Granada TV in 1966, working on *Coronation Street* as a floor manager. He subsequently joined BBC Children's Programmes, initially directing *Jackanory* with such stalwarts as Kenneth Williams, Bernard Cribbins, Judi Dench, George Lawton, Thora Hird, Christopher Biggins, Sue Pollard, Penelope Keith and Elaine Stritch.

Jeremy became the producer of the popular series *Rentaghost* and *Granddad* (starring Clive Dunn). He directed *Play Away* and the *Blue Peter* pantomimes. For Jim Henson Productions, he directed *The Secret Life of Toys* and for ITV, he directed *Art Attack*, *Sooty* and *Fraggle Rock*. In Australia, he worked on *Round the Twist* as a Producer and directed *The Genie from Down Under*.

He's still writing and painting – everything from walls to Christmas cards.

### Dr Paul Taberham

Paul is Senior Lecturer at the Arts University Bournemouth, and part of the Animating Minds consortium.

### Dr Tatyana Terzopoulos

Tatyana Terzopoulos is an Assistant Professor in the RTA School of Media/The Creative School at Toronto Metropolitan University and an expert in and passionate advocate for children's/youth media – factual and documentary media in particular. She is also an award-winning media creator, screenwriter, director and producer with over 17 years of experience across a range of genres on programs for domestic and international audiences. Her research and consulting work focuses on children's/youth media/media cultures; critical, ethical, and inclusive media education and media production practices/processes; and youth-centered research and media-production. She holds an MA in Communication and Culture from Toronto Metropolitan University and York University and a PhD in Language, Culture, and Teaching from York University. She currently teaches undergraduate and graduate level courses in children's/youth media and documentary production.

### Colm Tobin

Colm Tobin is a producer, writer and creator; and co-founder of Turnip + Duck, an award-winning creator studio based in Dublin, Ireland. With a background in law and music, Colm has worked over many years across productions from script to screen, attempting to balance creative work with figuring out how to get it financed. Together with Turnip + Duck co-founder Aidan O'Donovan, Colm has written over 100 comedy scripts, and created multiple original shows including *Brain Freeze*, *Critters TV*, *Atom Town*, and *Maddie + Triggs*.

### Dr Yalda T Uhlis

Yalda T Uhls PhD MBA, is a former movie executive (Sony, MGM) turned developmental psychologist and founding CEO of the UCLA Center for Scholars & Storytellers. An internationally recognized research scientist, educator, and author of the acclaimed book *Media Moms and Digital Dads: A Fact Not Fear Approach to Parenting in the Digital Age*, Dr Uhls has been named one of the top 100 people in Hollywood and one of nine experts changing Hollywood. She serves on several advisory councils, including NAACP's Entertainment Council, Common Sense Media's LA Advisory Council, and the YouTube/Kids and Family Council.

## Colin Ward

Colin is a lecturer in film and television production at the University of York and Deputy Director of the Children's Media Foundation with responsibility for the CMF's links with the research community. He is a former children's producer and director and started his career at Yorkshire Television, working across factual, entertainment and drama formats. He won a BAFTA for *The Scoop* before joining Granada Kids to produce the BAFTA-nominated gameshow *Jungle Run*. Moving to the BBC, he won a second BAFTA for the gameshow *Raven*, going on to work as an Executive Producer with CBBC Scotland.

## Nick Wilson

Nick Wilson's 45 years in Children's TV began at the BBC in 1974, working first on *Play School*, then *Chock a Block* and *Bric a Brac* before producing and directing on *Saturday Superstore*. From 1984–88, Nick was Editor of Children's Programmes at TVAM, where he created the *Wide Awake Club* and *Wacaday*. That was followed by a stint as Editor of Children's and Youth Programmes for Granada before setting up indie Clear Idea Television producing programmes for TVAM, ITV, Nickelodeon and the BBC. He joined the launch team for Channel 5 as Controller of Children's Programmes in March 1996, creating the highly successful preschool block Milkshake.

## Dr Ashley Woodfall

Ashley is an Associate Professor in Children's Media at Bournemouth University where he is Deputy Head of the Centre for Excellence in Media Practice (CEMP). With a PhD in children's media industries and audiences, his research interests span children's media experiences/culture and the children's media production landscape. Current research projects include a (British Academy funded) study into children's understanding of public service media and a (National Lottery Heritage Fund) community history project in which he is working with children as they create artwork and tell stories about their local town centre. Ashley is a member of the Executive of the Children's Media Foundation (CMF) and Co-Editor of the Children's Media Yearbook, as well as Editor of the Media Education Research Journal (MERJ). Ashley worked in television for many years before joining the teaching and research community, with experience that spans producing and directing factual, news, continuity, promos, commercials, entertainment and comedy – often with an interactive slant and mostly within Children's TV. His career began within MTV and LWT's camera departments, and he still very much enjoys picking up a camera (video or stills) when the opportunity arrives.

## Freya Woolford

Freya is a Research Intern at the Queen Mary University of London, and part of the Animating Minds consortium.